Tales from the Chicago Bears Sidelines

John Mullin

Sports Publishing L.L.C.
www.sportspublishingllc.com

Director of production: Susan M. Moyer
Project manager: Jim Henehan
Dust jacket design: Kenneth J. O'Brien
Developmental editor: Gabe Rosen
Copy editor: Cindy McNew

ISBN: 1-58261-648-5

Printed in the United States of America

Sports Publishing L.L.C.
www.sportspublishingllc.com

Contents

Acknowledgments

It is impossible to name all the individuals and sources who contributed to this work. Some of them are unknown; there are Bears tales tucked away in memories of everyone who ever followed, covered, played for or coached the team, and those stories always seem to start something like, "I always heard this one story about..." Where they first heard it they sometimes can't remember. Such is the way of lore and legend.

But some special thanks are in order nonetheless: to Hub Arkush, Greg Blache, Mike Brown, Rick Casares, Bobby Douglas, the late Hugh Gallerneau, Dan Hampton, Jim Harbaugh, Mike Hartenstine, Warrick Holdman, Jeff Joniak, Jack Karwales, Frank Kmet, Glen Kozlowski, Erik Kramer, Dale Lindsey, George McAfee, Dave McGinnis, Jim Morrissey, Ray Nolting, Ed O'Bradovich, Bryan Robinson, Marcus Robinson, Jim Schwantz, Ed Sprinkle, Tom Thayer, Bob Thomas, Tom Waddle, and James "Big Cat" Williams.

The Bears organization itself is due thanks and appreciation. The annual Fan Convention is full of stories and includes a session each year with ex-Bears in which fans can step up to the microphone and ask a player, "I always heard this one story about..." NFL Films also has done a superb job of preserving tales of the Bears and others for all time so that future generations can hear Butkus growl, watch Sayers and

Payton run, and enjoy the legends that never seem to grow old.

Colleagues and even competitors have my gratitude. Melissa Isaacson and Don Pierson of the *Chicago Tribune* made the job of storytelling and story-swapping fun, and Mike Mulligan of the *Sun-Times* helped keep fresh the memories of some special moments, usually with one of us starting off, "Hey, remember the time in Tampa when..."

No one book could ever hold all the great stories, and there are too many recommended tomes to list in one place. Mike Ditka's autobiography done with Don Pierson is a must for any Bears bookshelf, as are George Halas' *Halas on Halas*, Jim McMahon's autobiography done with Bob Verdi, and the books of Richard Whittingham, more recently his *What Bears They Were*.

This project never happens without the love and support of Kathleen Rude, who kept telling me I should write the stories down in one place and turn them into a book. Not long after she suggested that, Mike Pearson of Sports Publishing called with the same idea. Great minds do indeed think alike. And what book would be complete without help from Griffin, the Wonder Dog? No matter how old you are, if you still feel like a puppy inside, you get it.

Finally, thanks to the readers and listeners who are the real reasons I have a job. What's the fun of having great stories if you don't have someone to share them with?

Introduction

In Steven Spielberg's *Raiders of the Lost Ark*, archaeologist Indiana Jones battles to secure the Ark of the Covenant, the repository for the stone tablets given by God to Moses on which were inscribed the Ten Commandments. The Nazis wanted it for its supposed power.

Jones sought to find it as well but was most interested in keeping it from the Nazis. At one point Jones threatens to blow up the Ark with a bazooka.

Jones's adversary, a French archaeologist named Belloc, challenges Jones to go ahead, destroy the Ark. Jones can't. Belloc knows it, and knows why.

"Indiana," Belloc chides, "you and I are just passing through history. The Ark *is* history."

We as fans, media and others watch football history. The Bears in these pages *are* history.

The Chicago Bears are more than a football team. They are part of the civic fabric of a city and its people. Carl Sandburg was close when he titled Chicago as the City of Big Shoulders. He just didn't go far enough; Chicago is the City of Big Shoulder Pads. Chicago fans want to love their Bears because the Bears are much of what Chicagoans like about themselves: Big. Tough. Champions.

And characters. The Bears, like Chicago, are not just people. They are personalities, for better or worse. They have their mean side, their fun side, their quiet side, their tender side. Their stories. Their tales.

The history of the Bears is the history of pro football. Just about everything that could happen to a pro football team has happened to the Bears; just about everything that could happen to a pro football player has happened to a Bear. Or has been done by a Bear.

George Halas founded the Bears in 1920, not as the Bears and not even in Chicago. He and representatives of 12 other clubs met in Canton, Ohio, and worked out plans for their venture into professional football, which was no small gamble at a time when college football was king of the pigskin landscape.

It was the beginning of a litany of adventures, and sometimes misadventures, that would culminate in a sport that, if it couldn't be America's pastime (baseball had already laid claim to that honor), then it certainly became the king of America's sports interest. The Super Bowl trophy is named for Vince Lombardi, winner of the first two. It should be named for Halas, the man who made it all possible and on whose shoulders Lombardi and so many others would stand.

Halas was a Chicago native and three-time letter winner at the University of Illinois playing under legendary coach Robert C. Zuppke. Ironically, "Zup" would also coach Harold "Red" Grange, the player whose signing enabled Halas to truly launch pro football and enabled him to become a charter member of the Roaring '20s Golden Age of Sports. Zuppke advised Grange against signing to play pro football. Fortunately for Halas and America, he didn't have any more success stopping Grange in that effort than most defenders of the era had in stopping Grange with a football in his hands.

What brought Halas to that Canton meeting was a dream of Mr. Arthur E. Staley, who'd gambled on himself and eventually built a highly successful cornstarch manufacturing company in Decatur, a small town 175 miles southwest of Chicago. As a promotional vehicle and to build employee morale, Staley, through the company's Fellowship Club, sponsored the Staley Starchmakers, a semipro football club, and in March 1920 persuaded Halas to coach the team, which traveled to face other semipro clubs in the Midwest.

A problem with scheduling prompted Halas to write a letter to Ralph Hay, manager of the Canton (Ohio) Bulldogs and suggest forming a league. Hay had been thinking the same thing and already had met with representatives of teams from Akron, Dayton, Cleveland and Massillon, all Ohio towns.

On Sept. 17, 1920, representatives of the teams met in Hay's car dealership, in a showroom big enough for only four cars—Hupmobiles and Jordans—and formed a league that would far outlast those present that day, automotive and athletic. There wasn't enough room for chairs. Halas sat on a running board.

From that two-hour meeting, more than a dozen teams joined the new American Professional Football Association. Besides the newly named Decatur Staleys, there were the Buffalo All-Americans, Canton Bulldogs, Cleveland Indians (headed by the great Jim Thorpe), Dayton Triangles, Akron Professionals, Massillon Tigers (the city from which Paul Brown came and the nickname to this day of the local high school gridders), Rochester (N.Y.) Jeffersons, Rock Island (Ill.) Independents, Muncie (Ind.) Flyers, Chicago (Racine) Cardinals, and Hammond (Ind.) Pros.

Not all would even make it into the season that started Oct. 3 with Halas' team defeating the Moline Tractors 20-0, and through the years others would come and go from what Halas and the others created.

That first Halas team set a standard. In its 13 games (10 wins, one loss and two 0-0 ties), only three opponents scored, one being the Chicago Cardinals for a 7-6 win.

But in 1921 Staley told Halas that the company, while basking in the regional exposure the team gave its name, couldn't underwrite the expenses any longer. And Decatur was too small to support a professional franchise. He suggested that Halas take the team to Chicago, where it was drawing its best crowds, and staked Halas to $5,000 seed money, for salaries of $25 per week per player and other expenses, on the condition that Halas call the team the Staleys (officially "The Staley Football Club") for one more season.

Halas happily agreed, then struck a deal with Bill Veeck Sr., president of the Chicago Cubs, to use Cubs Park. Since the park wasn't being used after baseball season—some say it still isn't used much during baseball season—Veeck liked the idea and let Halas play there in exchange for 15 percent of the gate and concessions. Halas bargained back for the program rights, and the verbal agreement between the two stood for 50 years.

After that first Chicago season, the "Staleys" ceased. Halas wanted to show his appreciation for how Veeck and the Cubs had helped him and considered naming his team the Cubs. But he reasoned that football players were bigger, stronger and (except for maybe Ty Cobb) certainly a lot meaner than baseball players, so he went bigger with his name: The Chicago Bears.

Halas' team, like the football league he and the others started, became bigger in many, many ways. But underneath the glitz, the money, the celebrity, it was always still people: young men with fears, hopes and dreams, playing ultimately for themselves and each other.

It was that way in the beginning. Deep down, it still is.

Foreword

Author's Note: *The newest Bear to step into Pro Football's hallowed pantheon, the Hall of Fame, lived his professional life down amid the sound and fury of the trenches, where the game always was won or lost and always will be. Dan Hamption was voted to the Pro Bowl four times, twice as a defensive end, twice as a tackle, and was the anchor on one of the greatest defensive lines in the history of football. In his 12 seasons, "Danimal," as he was known by teammates and fans alike, played in 157 regular season games, starting 152, and was named defensive Most Valuable Player in 1982 by Pro Football Weekly. He was the fourth player taken in the 1979 draft following a senior season at Arkansas in which he recorded 18 sacks on the way to being named Southwestern Conference defensive player of the year. As long as there is football played in Chicago, they will tell stories of "Hamp," and the author is grateful not only to Dan for his own contributions to this collection, but also for his part in the stories told by others. More than one Bear, talking about his own experiences, insisted, "Hey, you have got to talk to Hamp. He's got the best stories, and besides, he's in 'em too!"*

*   *   *   *

When I was drafted by the Bears in 1979, I was horrified. That's the truth; like all young college players, I wanted to play in Miami, Los Angeles, San Francisco, anyplace warm. Little did I know that I was on a collision course with destiny.

In 1979 the Bears were going through a down cycle. Everyone knew of Butkus and Sayers and other greats.

But that was in the past, and even with Walter Payton here and a decent year here or there, the franchise was down. You almost felt that something of the greatness that had been the Bears was past.

All that was to change when, in one of his final acts, Papa Bear George Halas hired Mike Ditka because of his burning desire to rekindle the flame of the Monsters of the Midway. It didn't happen overnight, but within a few years, with great players like Walter, Mike Singletary, Richard Dent, Steve McMicael, Jim Covert, Mark Bortz, Jay Hilgenberg and others, we had returned the greatness of the tradition to the Chicago Bears.

It doesn't take long in the league to figure out what the Black and Blue Division was all about.

These stories weave in the tales of the greatness that went before with the rekindling that I was privileged to play a part in, and on into the years that followed. The stories are more than just stories. They define and reveal a little about the men who played this brutal game the way it was meant to be played, in a city where it was meant to be played, and in front of fans who are simply the greatest in any town or sport.

Dan Hampton

CHAPTER 1

THE JAURON ERA

Dick Jauron took over as Bears coach in 1999, beginning a tenure marked by upheaval and changes within the organization itself. The Bears changed presidents, added a general manager and went through quarterback changes on what seemed like an hourly basis. It was a time that left the Bears changed for all time.

Not My Fault

Quarterback Cade McNown made himself an outcast almost from the moment he arrived in training camp; not the way for a future leader to start off, particularly after being the 12th player taken in the 1999 draft. McNown was 11 days late after a contract impasse that was in fact not his fault (the Bears eventually gave him exactly the deal that agent Tom

Cade McNown ***AP/WWP***

Condon asked for at their first negotiation), but he wasted little time irritating teammates.

In one of his first practices, he rolled out the way he had at UCLA and cut loose a pass to wide receiver Macey Brooks, who happened to be covered by three defenders.

The ball was intercepted, after which McNown chided Brooks for running the wrong route. Not bad for a quarterback who was two days in camp and who'd been the one to cut the ball loose into triple coverage.

In his first preseason game he mishandled the snap from center Casey Wiegmann, now the starter for the Kansas City Chiefs, when McNown simply pulled back from the snap position too soon. McNown had pulled out too soon but blamed Wiegmann for not getting the ball back to him properly.

Because 1999 was his rookie season and Shane Matthews and Jim Miller were much of the quarterback story, McNown's growing problems were overshadowed, particularly because it was also the first Dick Jauron season and there were many events to occupy fans' attention. But the pattern was set for deeper McNown difficulties.

His already shaky relationships within the locker room worsened after a loss to the New York Giants in early 2000. One week earlier he'd been destroyed in a 41-0 loss to the Tampa Bay Buccaneers in the second game of the season, after which offensive linemen were furious over McNown's failure to get rid of the ball on time, his stupidity in the pocket, running his way into sacks, and not being prepared to recognize his responsibilities on plays, a problem that would be his ultimate undoing later in the season.

"He tells everybody in the huddle, 'Look out for the blitz,'" recalled tackle James "Big Cat" Williams. "He drops back and gets hit—BAM!—right in the mouth. We're walking to the sidelines then and he's cussing and fussing, 'Who's fucking guy was that?' We all said to him, 'That was the 'hot' guy. That was YOUR guy.'"

Against the Giants, McNown overthrew Brooks once and Marcus Robinson twice on wide-open deep passes where they were behind the defense. Afterwards, McNown put the blame on the receivers in a unique bit of subtle slam: "I think I just need to be aware that during the game those guys get a little tired and aren't running as fast," McNown told the postgame press corps.

The receivers were incensed at the not-so-subtle shift of blame for McNown's own bad passes. Robinson went to McNown privately and told him he needed to watch his mouth, that he was losing respect and tolerance among his teammates.

It got worse.

McNown hurt his shoulder at Philadelphia, after which the team picked up noticeably under Jim Miller and then Shane Matthews after Miller tore his Achilles at Buffalo. McNown sat out for six weeks, then was judged healthy enough to return. Mysteriously, coach Dick Jauron chose to start McNown at San Francisco right after Matthews had been near-perfect in a win over the New England Patriots.

McNown, despite having six weeks off to study and prepare for a fresh start after a 1-7 record in the games he'd started before the injury, effectively ended his Chicago career that week. Players said the practices leading up to the 49ers game were some of the worst they had ever been part of. McNown not only threw badly but did not know his assignments, reads or anything else. Clearly he had done nothing with his time off and was phoning it in at game 15 of a lost season.

Trouble was, the players were not quitting, even with their 4-10 record. They were determined to prove that they were not a bad team and that the main reason for their problems was McNown, and his performances Wednesday, Thursday and Friday at practice were proving it. At one point, offensive lineman Todd Perry approached Bryan Robinson and members of the defensive line and apologized in advance for the way they were looking.

On Friday afternoon, after the brief practice, the defensive linemen met for their regular Friday huddle. Instead of settling on one last 49ers point or scheme thought, they decided among themselves that above all else, they needed to go into Sunday expecting to play at least 40 minutes, because the offense under McNown was simply not going to stay on the field.

They were prophetic. McNown began calling nonexistent plays and protections for the line, mixing routes and blocking, failing to get his check-off calls correct. The game was a disaster, a 17-0 loss to the 49ers in which the play of McNown and the offense was overshadowed for the moment by Terrell Owens's record-setting 20 receptions.

"He didn't know what he was doing," Big Cat says. "He didn't know his audibles, would come up to the line and at one point audibled to a play that didn't exist.

We were up on the line saying to each other, 'What the fuck did he just say?'

"It was so bad that they asked Dick if he wanted to pull him out and Dick said, 'No, let him finish the game' It was almost like he was smirking and saying to management, 'You want this quarterback? I'll show you what you've got in this quarterback.'

"I think it was more to the people upstairs than to Cade. He already had his opinion of Cade."

Privately the players were enraged. The anger was not at Jauron, whom the players all believed was being pressured by management to play McNown, if for no other reason than to find out whether or not the kid could play, even though the locker room had long ago decided he couldn't.

There was talk that if Jauron insisted in starting McNown at Detroit, more than a few players simply did not want to take the field. McNown's lack of commitment and preparation put them at risk and made all of them look terrible as a group. Because of the players' respect for Jauron, a true rebellion and sit-down strike was unlikely, but as defensive back Frankie Smith and others said privately, "There would have been an awful stretch of 'slight hamstring strains' that week if they stuck with McNown for that last game."

Several players talked with Jauron and let their feelings be known. Jauron was not one to be pressured and the players weren't trying to do that. But Jauron also was a former player himself and knew what they were feeling, and that McNown did not deserve to play, not with a group that was still willing to play hard. Any

Dick Jauron ***AP/WWP***

rebellious thoughts were quelled when Jauron announced that Matthews would again start, and a Paul Edinger field goal gave the Bears a 23-20 win at Detroit, knocking the Lions out of the playoffs and giving the Bears two wins in their last three games and some momentum into next season's 13-3 season.

And McNown? He never made it out of preseason. He was called into a closed-door meeting with Jauron and quietly cut to ribbons for his conduct, unprofessionalism and failure to be an NFL player. When GM Jerry Angelo arrived in June, he familiarized himself with the McNown situation and had his own meeting with McNown. There he told McNown that the quarterback had "taken on too much water in Chicago and with this team." He began shopping McNown in trade and eventually dealt him to Miami for a late-round draft choice. Miami's personnel department was under Rick Spielman, who'd been the pro personnel director in Chicago when the Bears drafted McNown.

After a wasted season, McNown was sent packing, released and sent to the San Francisco 49ers–the very team against whom he'd show he had no business in an NFL uniform.

Togetherness

Offensive lines are traditionally one of the closest-knit groups on a football team, but the Bears took that to a new level. At one point before the

2002 season, the wives of center Olin Kreutz and guards Rex Tucker and Chris Villarrial all were expecting babies. Joked Kreutz: "We do everything together."

Blache Bullets

Defensive coordinator Greg Blache, whose hobbies include serious hunting, wanted to motivate his players to become more physical. He decided upon a reward system based on high-impact hits that involved presenting a player with one high-powered rifle shell for a major hit on an opponent.

The player who earned the most bullets during the season would receive a color television.

It worked. Players prized the gesture and lobbied for the bullets after big hits. Safety Rashard Cook, a 1999 draft choice who played only in preseason before being cut, still has his one Blache Bullet earned for huge hits delivered on kickoff coverage during the preseason.

The system came to light when cornerback Tom Carter, whom Blache rode hard because of Carter not being a more physical player, was cut in midseason. Carter had won precisely one Blache Bullet before his release, and when he cleaned out his locker, he left absolutely nothing in the stall, only the solitary bullet standing on the shelf, where the world could see it. It was his special "goodbye" to teammates, Carter said.

The problem was that the NFL doesn't allow teams to compensate players without it counting under their salary cap. The story on the bullets reached the NFL office, which promptly called Blache and told him to cease and desist, as did coach Dick Jauron. But not before the incident became a huge topic on talk shows in town, which unfairly portrayed Blache as some gun-toting violence monger in a time when guns and such had become such a huge issue for society.

Blache Watch

Dick Jauron's defensive coordinator Greg Blache rarely has kind words for the media. "You guys would find holes with Mother Theresa," he complained. "If it was up to you she wouldn't get into heaven because she didn't cure cancer."

Blache accused the media of leaking game plan information to the Baltimore Ravens before the Bears played them to open the 2001 season. His source of inside information? Television psychic Miss Cleo.

"Oh yeah, that's where I get my information," Blache deadpanned. "She's more informative than you guys are, I'll tell you that."

Muttered one press room wag: "Yeah, and she's probably a better defensive coordinator than you are, too."

Asked if he was having fun as a defensive coordinator getting ready to face the Minnesota Vikings with Randy Moss and Daunte Culpepper, Greg Blache shook his head: "No, no. I don't know what gave you that idea. The only thing B. B. King's got on me is guitar and sunglasses. I got the blues, trust me."

Things were getting so bad during a seven-game losing streak in 2002 that "we've been getting calls from Division II schools trying to schedule us for Homecoming," Blache moaned. "I turned them down because I didn't want to overschedule."

Bad Introduction

When Jerry Angelo arrived as general manager in 2001, he wasted no time in angering most of the team, which turned out to have good results, at least initially.

An introductory team meeting was called and coach Dick Jauron made his remarks, then invited Angelo up to address the team. Instead of a welcoming comment, Angelo shocked the room by essentially threatening everyone's job, beginning with Jauron. It was not a great start, given that Jauron had established a bond with the players, who felt he'd taken the fall for management the year before with the McNown fiasco.

The players were angry and there are those who believe a lot of the 13-3 mark in 2001 was their way of denying Angelo the chance to fire Jauron and bring in his own head coach. Others weren't so sure.

"It wasn't so much motivation as far as something he did, more of a 'Fuck you, really don't need you,'" says James "Big Cat" Williams. "Our big thing that year was we stayed healthy and didn't have a lot of people hurt. We had some good bounces that went our way. I don't think it had anything to do with Jerry.

"A lot of people want to say they played for Dick because Dick's job was on the line. He's a good guy, a player's coach; I can't take that away from him. But we were just on our game, we stayed healthy and were able to do what we wanted to do."

A lot of that started with a defense that played so well the offense could relax, and with an offense that went to Jim Miller after Shane Matthews was injured in the second game of the season.

"Everybody believed in Miller," Williams says. "He could come into the huddle and might say the dumbest shit as soon as he walks in, but you knew Jim was trying to get you going and he was 'real' about it. He's one of those quarterbacks like you see in the movies, where everybody is just ready to rally behind him. We know he doesn't have the strongest arm and he's not the most mobile guy. But we knew he was going to get up after a hit and he's not going to make a lot of mistakes."

Dance Fever

Minnesota Vikings defensive tackle John Randle found out that center Olin Kreutz was a native Hawaiian. The first time the Bears broke the huddle and Kreutz headed for the line, Randle broke into a hula dance that had the Bears' offense howling and almost calling for a timeout.

Less amused was running back Curtis Enis. He married a former exotic dancer and had to be restrained from going after Randle, who tucked a dollar bill in the belt of his uniform pants and as the Bears came to the line, yelled to Enis, "Hey, how 'bout having your lady do a table dance for us?"

Big Money

With all the money in sports, the numbers that get reported in the news can be pretty numbing. But what do you do, literally, with a check for millions of dollars?

Wide receiver Marcus Robinson signed a contract in 1999 that included a $5 million signing bonus. After taxes, that meant Robinson was handed a check for about $3.5 million at Halas Hall. What does someone do with a check for $3.5 million?

"I walked down the hall into DJ's [Dwayne Joseph's] office and sat down," Robinson said, shaking his head. "I didn't even look at it. I signed and they gave me the envelope. They gave me a folder for it, but I didn't want to be walking around with some folder in my hand, so I took the check and stuck it in the sleeve of my jacket, so I could feel it next to my skin.

"I walked straight to DJ's office. I said, 'DJ, open it.'" He knew I had signed but he didn't know how much. I went and bought a car, that day."

Fellow wide receiver Marty Booker had "number-shock" when he looked at his own signing bonus check. "I just opened it up, looked at it and went 'Wow, would I ever see this many numbers on one check?'" Booker marveled. "Oh, my goodness. I just put it in my pocket in case I needed security getting out of the parking lot."

Good Impression

Coach Dick Jauron was a former standout NFL player, a fact that was not lost on his players, who sensed in him an understanding of the little things that made pro football tough and thus an awareness of when to push and when to ease off.

Jauron also lived by "The Code" of playing the best player. If you were the best at your position, you played, not someone who was there just because he was a high draft choice. One exception was Jauron's playing of Cade McNown through the first half of the 2000 season despite it being obvious every Sunday and every day in practice that McNown was not the best at his position. The reason Jauron never lost the respect of the rest of the players: "We knew that Cade wasn't the best guy," says tackle James "Big Cat" Williams. "We knew it wasn't Dick [pushing him into the lineup]. It was the front office."

Jauron delegated full responsibility to his assistants and did not insist on hands-on coaching for himself. Instead, he was simply a presence that the players understood and appreciated, sometimes more than others.

"Dick will walk around all the time with this serious look on his face, and then walk up beside you and crack a little joke," Williams says. "A stupid joke, but it cracks him up. And you stand there and laugh because you have to, and then he'll walk off laughing, and two of you are standing there asking, 'What the hell was he talking about?'

"That was just him. He didn't talk to you that much like he was trying to buddy up or be one of the guys. But he is a good guy."

Rivals

The Bears-Packers rivalry is not the only one with some bad blood and tradition among the Bears. Former defensive end Trace Armstrong was once asked who his most-hated player ever was. "Tim Irwin," Armstrong answered immediately, identifying the long-time right tackle for the Minnesota Vikings. "If I ran over him with my car, I'd back up to make sure I got him."

The Vikings disliked the Bears back in the 1980s when a very talented Minnesota group was being upstaged by the Ditka Bears, not only for division titles but also for Pro Bowl honors. That dislike was fueled in 1998 when linebacker Dwayne Rudd returned a fumble recovery for a touchdown and backpedaled across the goal line with the ball extended, taunting running back Edgar Bennett, who was pursuing on the play.

But not all the "rivalry" thoughts are bitter.

"The only reason I really felt that rivalry was because of Korey Stringer," said defensive lineman Bryan Robinson, referring to the outstanding right tackle who died during training camp 2001. "That was my most intense, because we were both from the same state, I watched him come up and followed him through high school and I know he followed me. It was just an honor. "When I finally got to start, it was against Korey Stringer. Then the situation with him dying, it's tough for me to look at it like that now. They've got a different guy in there and, not saying Korey was better, but that was something special, we were good friends, and it was an honorable rivalry.

"We did talk off the field and were pretty good friends. That whole thing kind of screwed me up. And I was here when Dwayne Rudd did his thing and when they went 15-1. When we go up there, it's sold out and they hate the Bears.

"I don't think it compares to the Green Bay-Chicago rivalry because that's so old. But any team that's in your division, you want that extra edge to beat that team. And they hate you."

Looking Ahead

Few coaches have taken as much criticism as offensive coordinator John Shoop did in 2002. Injuries gutted the line and took No. 1 quarterback Jim Miller out for sizeable chunks of the season, but fans weren't interested in the problems; they wanted offense.

But even while players sometimes grumbled about excessive conservatism, they also understood that Shoop had a plan, like it or not.

"Shoop has to call his game, get to a point where he's comfortable calling his plays," says "Big Cat" Williams. "He won't score a lot of points early but he needs time. But you will have the opportunity to score points later because he is very good at making one thing look like another."

The McGinnis Fiasco: The Real Story

The disastrous hiring-then-not-hiring of Dave McGinnis to coach the Bears in 1999 was a turning point in the organization and led to the hiring of Dick Jauron. The McGinnis debacle led to the "firing" of Michael McCaskey by his mother and the installation of Ted Phillips as president of the team. But what really happened that day?

McGinnis was one of five finalists screened by personnel VP Mark Hatley and McCaskey. The others: Gunther Cunningham, then defensive coordinator for the Kansas City Chiefs; McGinnis, the former linebackers coach under Mike Ditka; Sherman Lewis, offensive coordinator for Mike Holmgren in Green Bay; Jauron, defensive coordinator at Jacksonville; and Joe Pendry, offensive coordinator at Buffalo and the Bears' running backs coach from 1993-94 under Dave Wannstedt.

McGinnis was McCaskey's first choice. He was popular in Chicago, and when Ed and Virginia

McCaskey visited the Phoenix area, they stayed with Dave and his wife Kim. So there was a special bond and comfort level.

That started changing almost from the moment McGinnis woke up on Friday morning, Jan. 22, 1999. First, based on Michael McCaskey's directives, the Bears put out a press release announcing McGinnis's hiring as the new head coach. It wasn't true; McGinnis hadn't worked out a contract, and in fact was in Chicago to get that done, but it wasn't a *fait accompli.* McGinnis heard about his hiring while he was shaving and getting ready at his hotel to meet with the Bears.

But the premature news announcement was not the real story of the disaster.

McGinnis was extremely upset at the news release but went to talk contract anyway. Significantly, McCaskey convinced McGinnis not to bring his agent with him, that the special relationship between McGinnis and the Bears made that unnecessary.

It turned out to be quite necessary. McCaskey immediately began playing hardball as the meeting got under way. The dollars were way below market rate for a head coach, and McGinnis several times was set to walk out. But finally the money was close enough to where McGinnis wanted on a four-year deal, and it looked like McCaskey would have his head coach in place after all.

But McCaskey in early 1995 had given Wannstedt a multiyear contract extension that shocked everyone. McCaskey was concerned that Wannstedt would be too hot a coaching property for him to afford if it came to bidding against other owners. Wannstedt had in fact chosen the Bears' top job over the New York Giants' offer when he left the Dallas Cowboys and Jimmy Johnson.

McCaskey hadn't negotiated a buyout into Wannstedt's deal and was on the hook for the final two years of Wannstedt's contract when he fired him, a $2.5 million hook. McCaskey was determined not to be in the same bind if things didn't work out with McGinnis.

So McCaskey wanted a clause that let him buy out the McGinnis deal after two years. Absolutely not, McGinnis said, correctly noting that such an arrangement made the contract basically just a two-year pact. Then came the dealkiller.

McGinnis: "And Michael, how can I convince assistant coaches to leave jobs or move families here for a coach with just a two-year contract?"

McCaskey: "Do they have to know?"

At that moment, McGinnis would say later, he knew he could never work for Michael McCaskey.

McGinnis would go on to succeed Vince Tobin, another Bears coach, the defensive coordinator under Mike Ditka, as coach of the Arizona Cardinals. McCaskey, rebuffed in his push for McGinnis, turned his attention to another alternative. He put in a call to Steve Mariucci, the head coach of the San Francisco 49ers and who was on vacation in Mexico, and got a final opinion on Dick Jauron. This time the agent, Don Yee, was involved in the negotiations, which were done by 9 p.m. after McGinnis had left to return to Arizona.

Dick Jauron was not McCaskey's second choice. Michael wanted then-Green Bay Packers offensive coordinator Sherman Lewis. Mark Hatley, whose first choice was Joe Pendry, whom Hatley knew from their days with the Kansas City Chiefs, was adamant that if McCaskey hired Lewis, Hatley would resign immediately.

The mutually agreeable compromise: Dick Jauron.

McGinnis's four-year contract started at about $800,000 and went up each year. The deal Yee worked out for Jauron was $1 million per season. So McCaskey lost money as well as his coach. And several weeks later, after the franchise was dubbed the laughingstock of the NFL, McCaskey lost his job.

Get to the Point

Middle linebacker Brian Urlacher is in charge of the defensive huddle, the eyes, ears and voice of defensive coordinator Greg Blache. But that doesn't mean teammates don't get a little scratchy with him.

The routine is for Blache to signal in the defensive call to Urlacher, who then silences all talk in the huddle—there's often a lot of it between plays, not all for family listening—with one word that ends all chatter: "Listen."

"One of the things that irks me about Brian," says defensive lineman Bryan Robinson with a laugh, "is that he'll know the huddle call and we'll be sitting out there during the timeout and I'll say, 'Did he give you the call?' And he goes, 'Yeah, I got the call.' And I'm like, 'Well ^%#$, give it to me, so I can get it in my mind, know what I'm going to do.'

"I'm always trying to get out of the huddle. I can't wait to get out. I've got to get this call and then I've got to walk around and dissect the play. Brian'll sit there and he'll probably be thinking of his child at home, some good moments, and I'm like, 'Excuse me, can you please give us the %$#@# call?'"

"Oh yeah," says Urlacher. "Yeah, B-Rob, I got it. Listen."

Getting Started

Brian Urlacher had been a safety while at New Mexico but starred at middle linebacker in the Senior Bowl prior to the 2000 draft, making that his projected NFL position. But the Bears weren't eager to just throw their prized rookie out at one of the game's most difficult positions, so they put him at the strong-side linebacker position, where his responsibilities would be primarily to play over the tight end and he could ease into the NFL game.

Urlacher lost that starting job to Roosevelt Colvin before the preseason was half over. But he would prove to be a far faster learner than anyone thought. When Barry Minter was injured in the second game of the season, Urlacher became the starting middle linebacker and never looked back.

Brian Urlacher *AP/WWP*

"He fooled us all," said Dale Lindsey, then the Bears' linebackers coach, now the defensive coordinator for the San Diego Chargers. "He caught on a lot faster than we thought he would. Anyone tells you different is lying to you.

"We started him at outside linebacker because that required the least amount of changes from college. We felt to take a rookie and put him at middle linebacker the first day training camp would be overwhelming. We didn't want to have what happens to quarterbacks put in there right away: lose confidence. But he kept showing us more intelligence, that he was more instinctive. We thought he could command respect."

"The difference between Brian and an average player, and it's the same with [perennial All-Pro linebacker Junior] Seau," says Lindsey, "is that Brian is so quick that he can screw up and still go make a play that the normal guy couldn't even make if he hadn't screwed up."

In the huddle, "we tell them put your hands on your knees and rest," Lindsey says. "Stare at the ground and be an idiot for a second, but when he says 'Listen,' we want your eyes up looking at him so you can hear and see him talking to you. That's what he does. He says 'Listen.' Everybody is alert; they know the defensive huddle call is coming."

Hearing Things

Because of their helmets, it's sometimes difficult for players to make out some of the conversations taking place on the field. Then again, maybe it's better that way.

"Somebody's cussing usually," laughs Brian Urlacher. "It's not nice. You might tell 'em, 'What are you doing?!' Most of the time you're yelling at them because it's so loud out there."

Urlacher gets his share of the yelling too. "One day in practice, I blew the call totally and did the wrong thing and Mike Brown yells, 'What the fuck are you doing?'" Urlacher says. "And I said, 'Don't get all moist, Mike,' which he always says.

"It's like, 'Shut up, dude. It's no big deal.'

"If you talk, then you're wasting your breath because you're going to get tired from talking too much. Just keep it short and have some fun. And this is a fun group right here, I'm telling you. All of the guys out there have fun.

"Walt [Harris] would say, 'Come on, Big Time.' He calls everyone 'Big Time.'

"Mike Brown will single out someone, even on his own team, even in practice. Once he says to Marty Booker, 'Book, if you step on me, I'll break your arm.' Just something stupid.

"The last time I was talking to the Minnesota Vikings center, Matt Birk, a little bit. He kept cutting my ass. I said, 'Hey, you're 300 pounds, why do you keep cutting me? You're bigger than I am.'"

Sometimes the talk has an edge, either mean-spirited or part of getting oneself to a higher level emotionally. "I'm always standing next to B-Rob [Bryan Robinson] and that's always interesting," Warrick Holdman says, laughing. "He'll say, 'See that guy right there? I'm going to beat him the next play. Look, he's scared.'

"You hear all kind of things during TV timeouts. There might be a guy on the other team you went to college with, you'll hear 'How's your wife doing? How's your little boy doing?' But then they'll blow the whistle and it's all right, now I'm going to try to beat you."

Levels of the Game

Players will tell you that the NFL game gets fast by levels and nothing in college can prepare you for what it is like. There is the shock of so much speed at the first minicamps right after the draft. Then training camp starts, when jobs are won and lost, and the speed jumps exponentially.

The first exhibition game, which for many will be the first time playing against another NFL team, takes the intensity to another level entirely. That happens again when the regular season begins and the games count. Waiting for the fortunate ones will be the playoffs and maybe someday the Super Bowl, played by the best against the best.

"It's fast and it stays fast," says Brian Urlacher. "Games are totally different. My rookie year I practiced and I was like, 'I got this, this isn't too bad.' Then you get in the game and it's so fast.

"It's like you're in the middle of traffic, because you have to weave around and avoid people. You don't want to get hit. I'm trying to avoid people. If I have to hit them, I will, but you really don't want to. You're just trying to go get the guy with the ball."

For linebacker Warrick Holdman, "It's like the first time I went to downtown Chicago and I was walking trying to find, say, the Water Tower and I was getting bumped, everyone is rushing past me and was just confusing. On the field, it's organized confusion. Everything is happening but all you can see is your man and what you have to do."

Multitasking at the NFL level carries into the rest of life too. "I can play Play Station, talking to my girl and on the phone with my mom," Holdman says, laughing. "I do that all the time."

CHAPTER 2

THE WANNSTEDT YEARS

After the Dallas Cowboys won the Super Bowl following the 1992 season, their defensive coordinator, Dave Wannstedt, was the hottest head-coaching prospect in the NFL. The finalists came down to the Bears and the New York Giants, with Dave's wife Jan ultimately voting strongly for Chicago as a better place to raise the couple's two girls.

Michael McCaskey pursued Wannstedt and hired him after Jimmy Johnson haggled for Wannstedt in a speaker-phone phone call with Wannstedt sitting there in the room while Johnson told McCaskey what Wannstedt had to have. It ultimately didn't work out for either McCaskey or Wannstedt. Some times were tougher than others.

Dave Wannstedt ***AP/WWP***

Blowup

The 1995 team had the most potent offense in franchise history, with Erik Kramer setting passing records throwing to Curtis Conway and Jeff Graham, and Rashaan Salaam rushing for more than 1,000 yards and 10 TDs as a rookie. They had reached the playoffs and upset the Vikings the year before and were off to a 6-2 start in '95.

But a porous defense and too many mistakes caused the season to unravel, reaching the low point in a bumbling 16-10 loss at Cincinnati that left the Bears 7-7. The blowup came the next morning and it was a monster.

The team watched special teams film all together, and everyone was in a bad mood. Special-teams coach Danny Abramowicz began to make prefilm comments but was cut off by coach Dave Wannstedt, who snarled, "Just run the damn film!" The film ran but with the room in silence, no coach making remarks, the first time any player could remember such a silence. When the film was finished, someone flicked on the lights and the order was given, "Go to your meetings."

Running back Lewis Tillman was outraged. "What the hell was that?!" Tillman yelled. The room turned to stone. Assistant coaches called for Tillman to shut up, but Tillman persisted with the question that was on everyone's mind: "Have you coaches quit on us?"

Order was finally restored but not before Kramer remarked, "It was unbelievable. It was like *The Exorcist*

Erik Kramer *AP/WWP*

where I thought stuff was just going to start flying around the room." The Bears won their final two games but still missed the playoffs when San Francisco was upset by Atlanta, and they did not have another winning season until 2001 when they went 13-3.

'Zo

Alonzo Spellman came to the Bears in 1992 as their No. 1 draft choice. He left in 1998 after one of the more bizarre Chicago careers ever.

Rarely was his tenure without some hitch. He'd gotten a hefty contract in 1996 when the Bears elected to match an offer from the Jacksonville Jaguars and fans held that against Spellman for some reason, that he wasn't worth the money. As Atlanta Hawk Jon Koncak once said after receiving a surprisingly large contract, "What am I supposed to do, give it back?"

As that 1996 season went along, Spellman's relationship with the Bears soured and spiraled perilously downward. He missed a Dec. 4 practice for personal reasons, but the team said the absence was not excused. When Spellman did show up, coach Dave Wannstedt felt betrayed after supporting the Bears' match of the Jacksonville offer. Wannstedt was critical of Spellman in front of the team and held Spellman out of the starting lineup Dec. 8 against St. Louis.

The situation worsened enormously when Spellman then asked for permission to address the team in private, no coaches. But instead of making the anticipated

Soldier Field ***AP/WWP***

apology for missing practice, Spellman contradicted Wannstedt's version of the situation. Wannstedt became incensed and their relationship deteriorated further.

It was on the way to becoming far worse. Spellman believed that the team had hired an investigator to look into aspects of his personal life, specifically the background of his wife, a mysterious figure in her own right, with stories beginning to circulate that she was involved in a voodoo cult, or some secret group.

If Spellman was becoming more and more distrustful of the organization, so were the Bears of him. Spellman, despite a well-known aversion to needles, suddenly began sporting unexplained tattoos. In the locker room before the Sept. 1, 1997 Green Bay game, Spellman appeared disoriented.

According to one story, Spellman was persuaded to attend a meeting of a voodoo group. There he was given a potion that rendered him unconscious, after which members of the cult pricked him with needles, drew some blood and mixed it into another potion, which they drank.

In one cataclysmic week in early '98, Spellman stormed through team offices, ranting and cursing after a meeting with Wannstedt. Several days later he appeared in the office of Ted Phillips and announced that he was retiring, a threat the Bears dismissed.

But the following Monday, Spellman was involved in what was treated as a hostage situation at the home of his publicist, Nancy Mitchell. The incident was resolved with the help of Mike Singletary and Spellman went to Lake Forest Hospital diagnosed as suffering from bipolar disorder, which produces wide extremes in behavior. His stay was brief, ending with him leaving late at night, wandering around in pajama bottoms and no top before police found him.

Trouble dogged the former No. 1 pick, although he did have stints with the Dallas Cowboys, where he had flashes of good play, and the Detroit Lions.

Ironically, the headlines behind his misadventures were drawing attention to the problem of bipolar disorder. 'Zo's difficulties, in the end, unquestionably helped others.

Checking Out

John Thierry was the Bears' No. 1 draft choice in 1994, the 11th player taken overall, which meant some big money for someone not quite used to it yet.

Thierry's rookie contract paid him a signing bonus of $2.5 million, the up-front money of the deal. Linemen Frank Kmet and Todd Burger were in the weight room lifting when Thierry, a country kid from rural Alabama, came in with an envelope and said he needed to know how to open a checking account.

Burger and Kmet along with other players received workout money, usually $500-$600. So Burger said sure and took Thierry's envelope and opened it as he told Thierry how to go to a bank, fill out a deposit slip and take it to one of the tellers.

Then Burger saw the check. "Holy shit!!!" he yelled.

The amount of the check Thierry was about to walk up to a new-accounts teller with: $1.3 million.

Bye-Bye

Character is always a difficult issue for NFL teams. The Bears, to their credit, have tried to steer toward players of character.

One player found that out in 1995. He was returning to his hotel room with a couple of ladies, neither of whom was his wife, and was on the elevator enjoying their professional talents when the elevator doors opened and Bears first family members Ed and Virginia McCaskey stepped into the elevator.

The player was a former Bear as of the next off season.

Disliked

Todd Sauerbrun was a second-round pick in the 1995 draft. He breezed into training camp with his "Hangtime" license plate and one of the strongest punting legs in the NFL, but one of the poorest attitudes from his teammates' perspecitive.

"I think Todd was the first person we put in a cold shower, took outside [naked] and tied up to the goal post in the snow," says tackle James Williams.

"Todd was an interesting character. He was a spoiled brat, still is. We were out at the Pro Bowl but nothing changed. A lot of times a guy will leave and go somewhere else, then figure out 'This is what I did wrong; I had a little personality glitch.' Todd will never figure that out."

The Watch

Frank Kmet was an All-American defensive tackle at Purdue after being the Illinois Player of the Year in 1988 at Hersey High School. But a broken leg in his senior season hurt his NFL chances after he was drafted by the Buffalo Bills in 1992. He eventually wound up with the Bears in 1993, where coach Dave Wannstedt and his staff decided that Kmet's NFL future lay on the other side of the ball.

Kmet went on the Bears' practice squad and eventually was put on the 53-man roster, in the vacancy created when the team released veteran guard Tom Thayer in midseason after Thayer returned from a back injury. A few days before the end of the season, Wannstedt went to Kmet and told him to start attending offensive line meetings now that he was an O-lineman.

Kmet went to his first meeting on Wednesday. On Friday, his third day as an offensive lineman, quarterback Jim Harbaugh came into the meeting room carrying 12 boxes. "Brought you guys a little something for Christmas," he said, passing out one box to each lineman.

The boxes were about the size and appearance of Kleenex boxes and "I thought, 'Geez, this guy's making a million bucks a year and he's giving out Kleenex? What a stiff.'"

Only they weren't Kleenex; they were Rolex watches, inscribed on the back with "Thanks. No. 4" and registered as official sports memorabilia.

"So here I am, on offense three days, and I'm getting this unbelievable watch," Kmet said. "I'm thinking, hey, this offense stuff is pretty cool."

A couple days later, Kmet's phone rang. It was Thayer, who'd blocked for Harbaugh.

"Hey, you got my f-ing watch," the caller growled.

"Tommy was always great to me," Kmet recalls. "So I want him to know that I'm taking good care of his watch."

Motormouth

The only thing more unstoppable than Minnesota Vikings John Randle's pass rush was John Randle's mouth.

A notorious trash talker with an outrageous sense of humor, Randle would study opponents' personal histories in their teams' media guides, and was rumored to occasionally have the book on the week's opponent on the bench during games. Sometimes against the Bears, though, he goofed.

Matched up against Bears guard Todd Burger, he harassed Burger about Burger's wife Jennifer, doing a little trash talking and taunting. Burger, normally a talker himself, didn't respond. After a few plays, Randle found out why.

"John," a teammate corrected, "Burger's wife is Denise. Jennifer is [left tackle] Andy Heck's wife." It was the only time the Bears remember Randle being at a loss for words.

Reggie

James "Big Cat" Williams came to the Bears as a defensive tackle, then switched to offense in the early 1990s. By 1994 he had earned his way into the starting lineup at right tackle, which put him on an annual collision course with Green Bay defensive end Reggie White, among the greatest ever to play the game.

Williams would hold his own in their epic battles. But the meetings were not without their doses of sheer terror.

"He wasn't the fastest but just enough that he could give you problems, and then [he had] that underneath move, that 'club' move," Williams says. "I remember before my first start against Green Bay, the Packers had played Dallas on the Monday night before. We were over at Curtis Conway's house, where we'd meet for *Monday Night Football* to eat, drink, cook, and we were sitting there a little after halftime.

"All of a sudden Reggie hit Erik Williams with that club-hook move and dropped him on his shoulders. The whole room got quiet and everybody looked at me. Somebody said, 'Damn, that's going to be you next week.' And it was my first year starting.

"Reggie didn't talk much. But we played on Halloween in that rainstorm in '94 and I was this feisty young guy, gonna make my mark, and I started with the, 'Hey, Superman, whatcha got today? C'mon, you ready to play today?'

"He didn't say a thing. He just raised his head a little and looked at me, and his eyes were red, blood red. I don't think I said another word to him the entire game."

Attention Getter

Mid-'90s safety Anthony Marshall was miffed at not starting. Asked what he thought he needed to do to convince the Dave Wannstedt coaching staff, Marshall mused, "I think I gotta put a bug in their eye."

Oooh, That Hurts

Linebacker Barry Minter, upset at a season-ending loss at Tampa Bay to the Buccaneers, sadly predicted, "A loss like that really sticks in your crotch."

Perspective

Chicago never quite seemed to embrace Jim Harbaugh completely, even though he guided the Bears to an 11-5 record and the playoffs in 1990 and 1991. Maybe it was because fans still savored the taste of Jim McMahon and Harbaugh replaced him as well as Mike Tomczak.

Whatever the reason, and whatever the perception outside of the huddle and locker room, Harbaugh was held in very high regard by teammates. He was tough, a leader, and took more batterings than outsiders knew.

"I thought the world of Harbaugh," says Tom Waddle. "I thought he was tougher and a better quarterback than people gave him credit for. He was negatively affected by Ditka, and I don't know if Mike was the right coach for him. But I know he was tough as nails and all the players admired him.

"We played two games back to back in '93 and he got sacked 18 times total, five times on three-step drops even. He was bruised, battered, bleeding, and came back and never once said anything against his O-line. We receivers probably didn't help him too much either. I know the system sure didn't help him. We were trying to run the Dallas Cowboys' vertical passing game and Wendell and I were 'horizontal' receivers."

'Zo

Defensive end Alonzo Spellman, talking about some bad breaks the Bears had been getting one season, observed, "We're 4-7 right now but we could just as easily be 5-3."

Tough Times

You knew things were bad and down to the bitter end when Spellman proclaimed, "It's time to circle the horses."

Spellman was memorable on the field, when he wanted to be.

"He could not work out for months and still look like a Greek god," said tackle James "Big Cat" Williams. "Then I met his sister and she's built just like him: ripped. It was just genetic. When we first met him, everybody said, 'Oh, he's got to be on juice, or something.' Then we started meeting family members.

"Our thing was, if we could have made 'Zo mad every Sunday, he'd be in the Hall of Fame right now. He was the most incredible athlete ever. We were playing Buffalo in '94, and on one play alone, he took a tackle with his right arm, shoved him off; took a guard with his left arm, shoved him off; hit the fullback, knocked him flat, and made the tackle. We said, 'Dude, if you could do that every day, you would be awesome.'

"And he could have. He just did not have the right attitude. In New England in '97, he ran the running back Curtis Martin down from 70 yards. He could do that any time he wanted to. 'Zo was just not that kind of athlete."

Welcome to the NFL

Curtis Enis' NFL career was short, generally unremarkable, and, well, colorful at times. His rookie year he was involved with the Champions for Christ group that included several teammates; his second year he arrived in training camp driving a black, chromed-up Hummer which he declared was just like him, "black and powerful," and after changing his number from 39 to 44, went several days with an extra 4 to become "444." His third year he was put at fullback and reduced to a minor role and wasn't re-signed after the 2000 season.

But his signature moment may have been his first day in '98 training camp. He had held out for 28 days in a convoluted negotiation between the Bears and his agent, and finally was in. Dave Wannstedt at that time had instituted a "bull-in-the-ring" contest before the afternoon practice, a one-on-one type of bout not seen in the NFL. Coaches brought the entire team together after calisthenics and before breaking up would call out one offensive and one defensive player, to meet in a circle formed by the assembled group. The two combatants went at each other on a snap count in a matchup that often served to put fire in the practice, at least for the winning-player's unit.

Enis came out for his first practice and was immediately called out. Against him: veteran linebacker Rico McDonald, a gentleman off the field but one of the most ferocious hitters and meanest members of the defense. Enis fancied himself a tough guy; the coaches yelled, "Go," and Enis was promptly on his back, looking out the earhole of his helmet.

He did pay the defense back the following year. Safety Ray Austin was angering offensive players with hits during camp, living up to his nickname "Advil" for the headaches he caused while with the New York Jets. On the last play of the last day of camp, Austin hit Enis, who'd had enough. He grabbed Austin, ripped off

Curtis Enis *AP/WWP*

his helmet and head-butted him, leaving Austin with a huge knot on his forehead and in search of some Advil.

Dangerous Man

Olin Kreutz became one of the best centers in the National Football League in a very short time. He established himself also as one of the toughest individuals in a sport of tough men.

"Olin doesn't give the impression, but he is one of the smartest players I've ever been associated with," says tackle James "Big Cat" Williams. "His bad-boy mentality, acting crazy, lot of fun—that's Olin, but he's probably one of the most studious guys I've played with. Olin is the most interesting guy I've played with.

"And Olin was not someone you mess with when he's upset. He has a little bit of a martial arts background, which makes him even more dangerous to go along with that attitude. He's into that kind of martial arts with some sort of grappling. So if Olin gets you on the ground, and doesn't like you, and gets hold of an arm, it's coming out. Separated."

Bad Welcome

In 1994 the Bears were trying to get to the playoffs and eventually would behind Steve Walsh, and would upset the despised Minnesota Vikings in the first round of the playoffs. But some of their toughest battles were not on the field.

Coach Dave Wannstedt believed in physical practices; the approach had served him well in stints with Jimmy Johnson coaching the Miami Hurricanes and Dallas Cowboys. But the Bears were starting to wear down in '94 and wanted to scale back the constant hitting in practices.

"We elected Trace Armstrong to go up and talk to him, tell him that 'We're a veteran team, we're near the end of the season and you're kicking our asses. Please back off in practice, the guys could use it,'" says Tom Waddle.

"I came in on a Thursday morning and I could hear this loud conversation happening as I'm walking in from the parking lot. I see Wannie and Trace going at each other, and I hear Wannie at one point say, 'Listen, if you don't think you can play for 60 minutes, I'll play Al Fontenot in there.'

"And Trace said, 'That's not the issue, Dave. The issue is that we're a veteran team and we need to back off a little bit. Guys are beat up.' Dave wasn't having any of it, and Trace was sent packing the following year."

Hated Guy

Denver defensive end Neil Smith may have been one of the NFL's best in his prime, but don't sell his act to tackle James "Big Cat" Williams.

"I hated that guy," Williams says. "He tried to poke me in the eye and tried to spit on me, and from that point on I hated him. A couple years after that I did an appearance for Spellman, a softball game, and then Smith comes over, all smiley, 'Hey, how ya doin'?' And I just told him, 'Hey, I don't want to talk with you.'

"I remember thinking, 'I would like to hit that son of a bitch with a bat.'"

"Rooks"

When Clarence Brooks arrived in 1993 as defensive line coach under coach Dave Wannstedt, his first position-group meeting included Trace Armstrong, Richard Dent, Steve McMichael, William Perry, guys with some time and experience. Brooks, in his first NFL job coming from the University of Arizona where he was an assistant, didn't make a great first impression when he opened by talking about the importance of hustle on defense.

Dent called him "Rooks," as in rookie. Brooks corrected him: "Brooks." "Right," said the Colonel. "OK, Rooks."

More Randle

The Bears went up to Minneapolis and John Randle, who always had a show ready for them.

His prime target: guard Todd Burger, a converted college defensive tackle with a temper and the one whom Randle most often lined up over.

During one timeout, the Bears were coming out of their huddle, the Vikings out of theirs, and all of a sudden, as they near the line, the Bears hear Randle yell to his teammates:

"When I say 'Burger', you say 'Bitch,'" recalls James "Big Cat" Williams. "And off he went with the rest of the Minnesota huddle yelling, 'Burger,' 'Bitch,' 'Burger,' 'Bitch,' 'Burger,' 'Bitch.' We lost it because it was something you never expected to hear. And he did it about five or six times. All we could do was laugh, and Burger was just pissed, red-faced, ready to kill somebody."

The Vikings in later seasons moved Randle out to defensive end. He was undersized at about 270 pounds and extremely quick, but the move to end wasn't easy. Williams and guard Chris Villarrial were the right side of the Bears' line and when Randle was out there, they got after him, cussin' him, punching him, cheap-shottin' him and getting in his face.

Then Randle jumped back inside to his more natural position of tackle and was over left guard Todd Perry. Perry came back to the huddle after Randle went to tackle, and muttered to Villarrial and Williams, "Hey, cut that crap out. Leave him alone. You don't have to play against him now."

Mr. Negative

Troy Auzenne was the Bears' second-round draft choice in 1992 and eventually became a starting left tackle during the Dave Wannstedt years. He was an excellent pass blocker from his days at Cal. But it was not his pass protection that made him the most memorable Bear to someone who saw more than a decade's worth of them.

"Most memorable was without a doubt Troy Auzenne," says tackle James "Big Cat" Williams. "He was the most negative person I've ever met in my life. Troy could talk you into a stupor. His locker was next to mine, and I've never met a person who, every day, just found something wrong. From the weather to the people, there was always just something wrong. He was a good guy. But I don't know what it was. Everything, EVERYTHING was negative.

"Troy could get to Tony Wise. He could stand around for 10 minutes just talking, about nothing sometimes, and Tony would be red-faced and ready to explode."

Chapter 3

DITKA AFTER XX

Iron Mike Ditka is second only to George Halas in the Pantheon of Bears coaches. Fittingly perhaps, it was the Old Man himself, who'd let Ditka go to the Philadelphia Eagles in 1967, who brought Ditka back in 1982 to restore the roar in his beloved Bears. It worked; the Bears had their only Super Bowl four seasons later and were back among the elite teams in the NFL for the better part of a decade.

How it happened: Ditka was coaching special teams for the Dallas Cowboys and had been thinking for several years about becoming a head coach. The only place he wanted to coach was in Chicago, so he wrote Halas a letter in 1981 in which he said: "I just want you to know that if you ever make a change in the coaching end of the organization, I just wish you would give me some consideration."

Halas did more than that. He hired Ditka in a deal struck around Halas' kitchen table, and the turnaround

began almost immediately. That turnaround would go through distinct phases: the makeover of the mind and personnel of the team; the 1985 season and Super Bowl XX; and the aftermath years.

Mike Ditka being carried off the field after Super Bowl XX.
AP/WWP

Super Bowl XX was a defining moment in Bears history, in NFL history for that matter, just like the '63 and '40 title games and other landmarks. Since then, however, a lot has happened...

* * * *

Mike Ditka's exit from Chicago traces to Oct. 4, 1992, in the House of Sound, the Hubert H. Humphrey Metrodome in Minneapolis and the home of the Minnesota Vikings. On that date, the 2-2 Bears were in complete control of the Vikings, leading 20-0 early in the fourth quarter, blessed with a first down near midfield due to a roughing penalty on the Vikings, who were demoralized and about to fold.

Then came the call that would change franchise history. Quarterback Jim Harbaugh came to the line with a pass called to running back Neal Anderson and flanked out to the left, hoping to create a mismatch against a linebacker on a surprise fly pattern down the field, a "Double-Seam" call with four receivers going deep.

But Harbaugh saw the Vikings' defensive alignment and decided to audible to a quick hitch pattern, with Anderson to drive off the line, stop and take the normally high-percentage short pass.

The trouble was, Harbaugh had been expressly ordered not to use audibles in the Metrodome because the din of the crowd made it virtually impossible to be sure all the players would hear the call, especially if they were away from the ball the way Anderson was.

"I don't think players were really listening for audibles," said offensive coordinator Greg Landry. "They might have heard but we really had stressed 'no audibles' to them so it may have been that they really weren't paying attention because we weren't calling audibles."

"It was the last thing we discussed [before Harbaugh went on the field]," Ditka said. "The very last thing. If it hadn't been discussed, I wouldn't have a problem."

Harbaugh yelled out the change, Anderson didn't hear it and broke down the field as Harbaugh made his quick drop and threw to where Anderson would have been on the hitch.

Instead, the ball was intercepted by Minnesota safety Todd Scott, who had no one in front of him and went untouched 35 yards for a touchdown. When Harbaugh returned to the sidelines, Ditka went berserk. He lambasted Harbaugh verbally, stalked away, then came back with another blast of rage.

The Vikings suddenly came alive, as did their fans, and rolled off two more scores for a 21-20 win. The loss fueled Ditka's fury. "Audibles are part of the game," he said. "But audibles are to get from a bad play to a better play, not from a good play to a worse play. We went backwards."

Most of the players indeed weren't expecting any audible, certainly not in that situation.

"We went into the game and Ditka had a mandate: no audibles," says Tom Waddle. "Because of the noise, we are not going to audible, regardless. If we send in a play that doesn't look like it's going to work, eat it. If it's a pass play, throw it out of bounds. Just hold onto the football. But we're not going to audible."

"The funny thing is that the audible was the right call, in another situation. But Neal wasn't looking for an audible because we'd been told we're not going to. Jim audibled to a 'hitch' and Neal kept running, Todd

Scott picked it and ran it back for the touchdown. The irony was that it was a good audible, just not an approved audible."

The incident refused to go away. The Vikings game was followed by a bye week, so after a week of questions upon questions, Ditka and the Bears went into Monday getting ready to look ahead for the Oct. 18 game against Tampa Bay. But The Audible refused to die and it was about to take Ditka down even further.

At the Monday press conference, the first question was not about the Bucs, practice or anything else. It was about The Audible. Ditka blew up.

"We've had probably 400 plays this season," Ditka said, seething. "And all you sons of bitches can talk about is one damn play."

Phil Theobald, veteran columnist for the *Peoria Journal-Star*, wasn't in any better mood than Ditka. "Coach," Theobald said, standing up from his desk, gathering his papers and walking out right past Ditka and the podium, "I have been insulted by enough people in my time and I told myself the last time Bobby Knight did this kind of thing that I wasn't going to be called a son of a bitch ever again."

The room, and Ditka, were floored. Finally, Ditka stammered, "Fine." Theobald left, and less than three months later, so did Ditka.

Not a Harbaugh Fan

Mike Ditka's relationship with quarterback Jim Harbaugh ended on a national stage with that famous blowup in the Metrodome, Ditka in Harbaugh's face over changing a play call. But their association didn't get off to an especially great start either.

Ditka in fact argued strenuously against drafting Harbaugh in the first place. Ditka was never one to spend too much time scouting college players, but he was big watcher of college bowl games when he had time. He had seen Harbaugh not play especially well in a Michigan bowl appearance at the end of the 1986 season and concluded that Harbaugh was not a big-game player.

When draft day arrived, Ditka wanted defensive end/linebacker Alex Gordon. Player personnel chief Bill Tobin wanted Harbaugh because of concerns, for good reason, over the health of Jim McMahon. Michael McCaskey cast the tiebreaking vote and Harbaugh became only the second quarterback drafted by the Bears in the first round in 36 years.

What Might Have Been

Players on the Super Bowl team savor the accomplishment but almost to a man believe they should have made it to more than one final game. Nowhere was that feeling stronger than in 1986 when the Bears went 14-2 and set an NFL record for fewest points allowed (187).

The problem was at quarterback. Jim McMahon couldn't stay healthy, Doug Flutie was brought in, and disaster followed in the form of a playoff upset loss to the Washington Redskins.

"All our people were hurt and they decide to bring Flutie in, that he'll be our starter," says Mike Hartenstine. "They couldn't just put Flutie back there in the pocket because he was too short, so they had to roll him [out] and now our offensive linemen have to learn all new blocking assignments and techniques for the game. For that one game.

"When I really knew we were in trouble was when [offensive coordinator] Ed Hughes was sitting in the locker room before the game. Ed is signaling Flutie the plays the way he would be in the game. He signals about 20 plays and Flutie got maybe two right out of 20. And I'm sitting there thinking, this is going to be our starting quarterback for the game?

"Granted our defense didn't do great, but I'm thinking I can't believe this, two out of 20 plays right."

War Games

The situation in the Middle East was deteriorating in '91 and several Bears were talking about it in the weight room. One was guard Mark Bortz, a serious student of warfare, and the question was put to Bortz: What do you think the percent chances are of us going to war in the Gulf?

"Probably 70-30," Bortz surmised.

William Perry saw it differently. "I think it's more like 75-35," Perry said.

"Fridge," one teammate pointed out, "that's 110 percent."

Fridge reflected, then emphatically declared, "Well, if you go to war, it SHOULD be 110 percent!"

Coverage Sacked

Donnell Woolford was one of the Bears' two first-round picks in the 1989 draft and he was an instant starter and eventual Pro Bowl cornerback, one of the Bears' better pass defenders in the 1990s. But his time with the Bears and coach Ditka got off to a very rocky start.

After a Bears loss late in Woolford's rookie season, Ditka announced publicly that Woolford "apparently can't cover anybody."

Harsh words for a young player on a team that was floundering for more reasons than his coverage. But Woody "took it more or less as a challenge," he said. "I didn't understand it at first because when you come up from college, people say things that maybe they don't mean. Ditka's comments really went in one ear and out the other, but it was shocking for a coach to say something like that about a player. Then I found out that's the way he is, so I don't even think about it.

"Except," Woolford said with a sly smile, "I knew it wasn't true. If it was, they wouldn't have drafted me."

In Awe

Think that NFL players are used to seeing stars and aren't affected by what they see around them? Maybe. But not if it was Mike Ditka.

"I remember driving to Halas Hall and walking down the stairs to the meeting rooms and just being terrified because of all the stars who were there," says Tom Waddle. "It was like you died and went to football heaven, with Dent, Hampton, Singletary, that offensive line, and then Ditka walks in. You don't ever forget that."

Not that Ditka was without flaw in how he ran things. Indeed, one of his strengths—loyalty—arguably was one of his weaknesses, too.

"Mike was loyal to a fault and probably stayed with guys longer than he should have," Waddle says. "But that was just the way he knew. So what would happen is he would keep guys on maybe a little long and then say things about them when things didn't work out, which burned him anyway."

Alienation

Mike Ditka brought the players together after his arrival in 1982. He transformed the mood, the chemistry, the physical makeup of the team and fused it into a potent club to wield against the rest of the NFL.

But five years later, he lost many of them. The strike of 1987 sent players out on an informational picket line and the Bears brought in replacement players, the so-called "Spare Bears." While Buddy Ryan in Philadelphia was contemptuous of the replacement players with the Eagles, Ditka declared that the "real Bears" were the ones wearing the uniform on Sunday.

After the strike was resolved and went away, the residue of perceived betrayal did not.

"In '87, he alienated certain players," says Dan Hampton. "It's like in a marriage, if you find your wife is cheating on you; you can stay together but it'll never be the same again. It was never the same again. Even though we had the best record in football in '88, it wasn't the same. By 1989, we were getting to the point of being exposed, and by '90 we were old and beat up, just meaner than everybody else, so we won the division, but that was it."

How Big Cat Became "Big Cat"

"The first time I came up to the Bears after signing as a free agent in 1991, Dave McGinnis, who was our linebackers coach, and Ditka were standing out in front of Halas Hall," James

Williams recalls. "When I got out of the limo, Dave said, 'Damn, that's the biggest cat I've ever seen in my life.'

"Somehow that stuck and I became 'Big Cat.' Now I wouldn't be surprised if half the young guys on the team didn't know my real name."

"Overachievers"

Mike Ditka was sometimes without equal as a motivator. Other times...

After the 1991 season, which ended with a 52-14 annihilation at the hands of the reviled 49ers, followed by an upset loss in the playoffs to Dallas, Ditka perhaps unwittingly alienated his players for what would prove to be a disastrous last time. He made a comment after the season that a lot of the players were "overachievers" and that he was "just playing the hand I was dealt," which many interpreted as a slap at team president Michael McCaskey and personnel chief Bill Tobin, with whom Ditka often feuded. Unfortunately the players were the ones who felt stung.

"If you have a coach saying, 'These guys are sending me a bunch of overachievers' and 'this is the hand I'm dealt,'" said quarterback Jim Harbaugh, "there's not a lot of harmony there, you know? There's no doubt about it. Guys talked about that a lot."

Not nicely either.

"It's kind of a slam," Harbaugh said. "Tom Waddle is a good player. How is he an overachiever? You're either good or you're not. It's tough to read that 'You guys aren't that good' or 'You're the hand that I'm dealt,' then turn around and tell us, 'Hey, you guys really are good. Let's go out and win this game'. It's a contradiction at the least. Why do you make those two different statements?"

"It's convenient," Harbaugh said. "If you lose, it's 'I didn't have the players.' And if you win, well, 'I motivated 'em.'"

Iron Mike didn't earn himself locker-room points either with a scathing comment in the Halas Hall hallway during Pro Bowl voting earlier that season.

"Nobody here can [urinate] in the direction of the Pro Bowl," Ditka growled.

Shouting Matches

Mike Ditka got into his players' faces. And they occasionally got into his. Ditka the ex-player didn't have a problem with that.

"I don't know how many times I was in the middle of a fight between 'Horne and Ditka," says Tom Waddle. "Those guys would have to be pulled apart on the sideline. They would be screaming and m-f'ing each other and afterwards 'Horne would go back to him and say, 'Coach, I didn't mean anything by that.'

"And Ditka would say, 'Hey, what happens on the field stays on the field.' And how refreshing was that?"

Seeing Is Disbelieving

The 1988 playoff meeting between the Philadelphia Eagles of Buddy Ryan and the

Former Bears Mickey Pruit (52) and Maurice Douglass (37) celebrate in the fog during the famed Fog Bowl, a 1988 playoff matchup in which the Bears defeated the Eagles at Soldier Field. ***AP/WWP***

Mike Ditka Bears was memorable for many reasons, but the main one was that no one actually "saw" the entire game.

The game, won by the Bears, has come to be known in NFL lore as the Fog Bowl, for the lakefront fog that rolled in during the game and obscured most of the action from the fans and even the players in some instances.

"The Fog Bowl was unbelievable," says Dave McGinnis, now coach of the Arizona Cardinals, then the Bears' linebackers coach. "You couldn't see anything. It was such a surreal feeling. Plus it was a big game, and you had Buddy coming back. There were so many elements to it and then for the fog to come rolling in over the south end, it was an unbelievable feeling.

"The further and further you get away from it....We've got Louis Zendajas on our staff in Arizona, and he kicked those four field goals for Philadelphia. He and I laugh about that game a lot. He's got a huge picture of him kicking a field goal into 'the white.' You can't see anything."

Hanging On

Wide receiver Tom Waddle is a classic Bears success story. He was an undrafted free agent out of Boston College, discovered and signed by scout Rod Graves, who would go on to head personnel for the Bears and eventually become general manager of the Arizona Cardinals. But it wasn't a straight line into the NFL once Waddle started out.

"I had three really strong camps in '89-90-91," Waddle says. "But when you make it to the last cut, Ditka would tell you, 'This is the hardest time, but when you come the next day, bring your playbooks because not all of you are going to make it.'

"When you'd drive down Washington Rd., you learned quickly that if your position coach was standing out there on cut day, you were in trouble. In '89 I pulled in and kind of expected to see my guy there. In '90 I didn't know if he was going to be there, and he was. In '91 I was sure he wasn't going to be there, and he was.

"I would go up the steps, and there's this L turn in the stairs. And I had this irrational fear that not only was Ditka going to cut me, but he was going to jump across the desk and beat the shit out of me. So I would go into the office prepared not only to get cut, but also to get beaten up by the coach, for some strange reason. I have no idea what that was all about; I just remember going into his office shaking.

"The third year he cut me after being the leading receiver in camp and I went up there ready to whip his ass, because I knew he was going to cut me. Obviously that wasn't possible physically and a good move for my job. He cut me but told me I was going to be back on the roster because Wendell Davis is going to go on IR.

But in Waddle's first game ('91) he was on the sidelines, admiring the game, and admiring himelf in uniform as the game was going on. He was waving to his brother halfway through the second quarter when it happened.

"WADDLE!" Ditka roared.

Startled, Waddle ran over and got the word: "You gotta go in," Ditka commanded.

"WHY?! WHAT'S WRONG?" Waddle yelled in disbelief.

"Anthony Morgan is hurt and we don't have anyone else," Ditka said, ending the discussion.

"That was an inauspicious beginning to my career," Waddle says.

Life Savers

After Mike Ditka had his heart attack, Hampton and Steve McMichael got into his best cigars and liquor cabinet. The two went through a number of vintage vices over a period of time. Finally Ditka came back. But that didn't deter the two miscreants.

"What are you two doing?!" Ditka challenged when he came back and found the two in his office puffing on two of his best stogies.

After a long pull on the Cubans: "We're saving your life," they answered.

Jimmy, What Were You Thinking?

By mid-1988, quarterback Jim Harbaugh was getting restless. He was the Bears' No. 1 draft choice the year before but wasn't getting on the field much behind Jim McMahon and Mike Tomczak. So he came up with another idea.

He began badgering special teams coach Steve Kazor, insisting that he wanted to get out on the field and cover kicks.

"That idiot," says Glen Kozlowski. "He's got the gloves on, getting all psyched up and ready to be the tough guy. I was out for a play after hurting my knee on the previous punt, so I isolated on Harbs.

"He's going down the field yelling like a madman, and he gets just jacked. I mean, jacked. Somebody blindsides him and he goes flying through the air all the way out of bounds. His helmet's turned around and he's looking out the earhole.

"Ya' know, Harbs never chirped about covering kicks again."

McMichael–Weird, Or...?

"The most eccentric teammate by far—and I'm sure he's going to get all the votes—is Steve McMichael," says receiver Tom Waddle. "Cap [Boso] was a space cadet, just kind of out there, a great player who worked his ass off. But you'd be in the middle of a deep conversation with him and all of a sudden he'd look at you and say, 'Do you find me sexy?' Just whacked out stuff like that. 'Absolutely, Cap.'

"But I didn't speak to McMichael for two years out of fear and respect. I got there in '89 and don't think I talked to any of the veterans until I stepped on the field. I just stayed out of their way, kept my head down and walked past guys as fast as I could. It was truly an era when you didn't speak unless you were spoken to. You remember the days when McMichael recognized you and said, 'Hey, kid, how are ya?' Of course, there were some expletives thrown in.

"He was eccentric in a good way. As strange as it sounds, he was kind of a stabilizing force for our team. He was someone everyone looked to in a tight situation to make a big play. The greatest example of that was stripping Blair Thomas of the football against the Jets on Monday night. They were running out the clock, Pat Leahy missed a short kick, and with a minute and a half left, Thomas went through the line, McMichael just reached around and ripped the ball out."

Ming

Steve McMichael was one of the most colorful Bears of the 1980s and early '90s. He'd been cut by the New England Patriots and picked up by the Bears and Ditka, eventually having the last laugh on the Pats by helping destroy them in Super Bowl XX.

"Ming," a hardscrabble Texan, was great on camera and a really intelligent guy. When he got on camera he understood that for notoriety, he had to push the envelope a little bit and he did. So he really developed a schtick and a persona that was signature.

But Steve was "the best football player that I ever played with," says Trace Armstrong. "Steve had great ability, but he didn't have dominant ability, yet he was a dominant player for a long time. He did it by working at it.

"I played with Steve for five years and he never missed a practice. They would drain 60 cc. of fluid off his knee Wednesday morning and he'd be out there practicing Wednesday afternoon."

McMichael enjoyed some off-field celebrity as part of the media he so richly despised, culminating with his installation as a color(ful) commentator on Channel 5, the NBC affiliate. That gig ended after a series of hijinks that included the on-camera snipping of host Mark Giangreco's tie with a pair of scissors.

"Steve was probably one of the toughest guys I ever played with," Armstrong says. "But he had this Hollywood style, too. He bought a Rolls-Royce convertible, red with a white interior and a white top. I'm going in to work one morning and here comes this red convertible, big guy driving with long hair flapping in the breeze, and this little chihuahua he's holding as he's driving.

"And the chihuahua's got some kind of outfit on. That was vintage Ming."

More Ming

"We've got leaders," cornerback Lemuel Stinson said during a difficult stretch of 1992. "Steve McMichael is a leader in his own way. Violent, but a good leader."

Jim McMahon *AP/WWP*

Turncoat

Jim McMahon left the Bears and wound up with the San Diego Chargers when they faced the Bears in a 1989 preseason game. In the second half, Bears quarterback Jim Harbaugh noticed that signal-caller Mike Tomczak was signaling Bears offensive plays. But he wasn't signaling them to the Bears' offense on the field.

Harbaugh looked across the field and saw McMahon standing next to the Chargers' defensive coordinator and he blew up.

"I said, 'Hey! What are you doing?'" Harbaugh says. "Tomczak just sort of blustered and flustered, saying, 'Hey, it was only for one play. Big deal.' But I could never figure out what he was doing that for or why. I still don't know."

First Impressions

James "Big Cat" Williams was a Bears fixture for more than a decade, an undrafted free agent who came in as a defensive tackle and left as one of the all-time great offensive linemen despite playing on poor teams. But he had to overcome some tough first impressions of teammates.

"I hated McMichael when I first got there, but he kind of grew on me," Cat says. "He and Mark Bortz I thought were just the biggest rednecks."

"It took me a while to realize what kind of guy Bortz really was. He was smart. He was a lot smarter than I thought he was at first, and when I first got there, I thought he was just the dumbest country redneck I'd ever met in my life. I think I was just waiting for him to slip up and say 'nigger' one day.

"Bortz knew how to push the little buttons. He never overstepped the bounds but he knew how to push you and get on your nerves. He didn't mean anything by it; it was just him. And once I got to know Bortz, Bortz was all right.

"McMichael was a little different. I never knew where he was coming from. He was old-school, said what he wanted, did what he wanted, and I found it interesting as well as obnoxious. He thought he was a little smarter than everybody else, 'You can't tell me anything. I can do everything.'

"He just walked around with his chest puffed out with that little ugly damn dog. He'd unzip his jacket and that stupid dog's head would poke out. I just wanted to crush that stupid dog. I didn't hate the dog; I hated him with the dog."

Tight Fit

Tight end Jim Thornton earned the nickname "Robocop" for his physique, which he didn't mind showing off. But it sometimes required some creative wardrobe management.

Robo found out that he needed a collared shirt for a function when he arrived at Glen Kozlowski's house. Koz told him to go up and help himself to anything in his closet that fit.

"Robo came back down with a shirt that I must have worn when I was in 10th grade when I was probably 110 pounds," Koz said. "I mean, it was like that shirt was painted on."

Jim Harbaugh offered a suggestion. "Robo, you were supposed to go in Koz's closet, not his kid's."

Remembers Koz: "And my oldest was six or seven at the time."

"Open the Damn Door!"

Ron Rivera and Glen Kozlowski were roommates in Platteville. One night Dan Hampton was among those coming back well after curfew, when the doors were locked and you'd probably get fined for coming in late. Hampton started tossing pebbles at the window to get them to come down and open the door for him.

The pebble tapping finally woke the two up. They looked down and saw Hampton. "[Screw] you," they said. "We're sleeping."

They went back to bed and a minute later the window shattered as a huge rock came flying in, glass everywhere.

"Get down here right now and open the g— d— door!" Hampton roared.

"We went down and opened the door for him," Kozlowski says. "Right away.

"And the beauty of the whole thing is that he wasn't going to practice then. He'd just sit around in those stupid football pants cut off like shorts and T-shirt that he cut the sleeves and waist out of and wore the shorts really high."

Tough Crowd

It wasn't especially easy to break in with the Bears of the 1980s and even when you did, it could be rough. Tom Waddle was trying to make the team as an undrafted free agent rookie, and during one wide receivers meeting, Waddle spoke up and asked a question about what coaches were explaining.

"What do you care, rookie?" veteran Dennis McKinnon challenged. "Your ass is gone in a week anyway."

Waddle did more than survive the week. He came back from being cut more than once and went on to be one of the most productive receivers in Bears history, with 173 catches.

McKinnon would finish with 182.

Medical Marvel

Cap Boso was running a really bad fever one night and got dehydrated. So he hit upon the idea of filling a bathtub with ice and water to try to break the fever. He jumped in and immediately became one giant cramp. The cramping caused him to hunch forward so that suddenly his nose and mouth were under water and he was about to drown. Fortunately he got out of the tub and into a hospital.

Hamp Knows He's Done

Dan Hampton had a long and distinguished Bears career, beginning as the fourth overall pick of the 1979 draft and finishing in 1990. When the end came, he knew it.

"Alan Page would say everybody's a beanbag. Every time you go out and lay it on the line, you take out one bean. Sooner or later, you're out. That's how I was at the end of my career. At the end of it, I could not have played one more quarter. That was the way I wanted it. I was out of beans."

The beans ran out against the Raiders in 1990.

"They kept pitching the ball and going left, and I'd never been hooked in my entire life, and [guard Steve] Wisniewski kept hooking me. He got to the shoulder about four times and drove me off the ball two or three yards, which I'd seen other people have happen, but I'd never had that before. That was like sticking a knife in me. I thought, I'm done.

"I remembered back when I came in and Tommy Hart, a great speed rusher, was through and people saying 'the old gray mare ain't what she used to be.' Well, I was the old gray mare. I could not believe I could be hooked."

Celebrity Status

Tight end James Thornton was among the more recognizable Bears, if not for his facial features, certainly for his biceps and forearms, exceptional even in a world of large limbs. Such were they that they earned him the nickname "Robocop. And he didn't shrink from displaying them, in a manner of speaking.

Robo was driving with a few teammates in the car one evening when a car full of fans pulled alongside. "Robo, Robo," they called out, trying to get Thornton's attention. Finally Robo rolled up the window of the car, muttering, "I hate all this attention they start paying to you," Thorton complained.

"Well," chided receiver Glen Kozlowski, "maybe if you didn't have 'Robo 80' as your license plate..."

The boys were at a hockey game and fans kept coming over to Robo for autographs. "I wish they'd stop asking for autographs," Robo complained.

"And he was wearing a jacket with 'Robocop 80' on the back! I looked at him and said, 'Are you going to make me say it again?'" Koz said.

Not-So-Offensive Lineman

The Bears' offensive line of tackles Jim Covert and Keith Van Horne, guards Tom Thayer and Mark Bortz, and center Jay Hilgenberg was arguably the greatest in franchise history. Bortz, Covert and Hilgenberg went to Pro Bowls and were the core of the NFL's dominant power rushing offense of the 1980s and into the early 1990s. And each had his own personality.

"I used to stand in the huddle next to 'Horne and he'd get tired and lean on me," recalls Tom Waddle. "So you've got this six-foot-eight behemoth leaning on my little six-foot, 180-pound ass and it looked crazy. I thought I had a great rapport with those offensive linemen because I was the same kind of athlete as a lot of them, which wasn't great. So we had this mutual respect level.

"I never wanted to leave the field because there was someone like Mark Bortz there who played with a muscle completely pulled off the pelvis in his groin. Most people would have had to be sedated and spend time in the hospital. He's out there grinding it out. I get hit and who am I not to come back to the huddle when you've got this guy doing that?

"He would never acknowledge that he was hurt. He had too much pride and was too tough a guy. He didn't say a whole lot. He just kind of grunted.

"They all were tough in their own way. Bortz didn't really want to fight you. He just wanted to beat you up from whistle to whistle, and he did a great job of that. 'Horne was someone who wouldn't take any grief from anybody.

"Jay was kind of the quarterback of the line. Bortz and 'Horne were the enforcers."

Game Misplans

Da Coach and offensive coordinator Greg Landry sometimes bickered over playcalling. But they weren't the only ones.

"It seemed like a lot of people weren't on the same page—Greg and Mike, Greg and [receivers coach] Vic Rapp, Greg and Johnny [Roland, running backs coach]," Harbaugh says. "It seemed like it was different things all the time. Everybody had different ideas how they wanted things to work. I don't think everybody agreed on the right way to do things. It created problems.

"During the week, you'd practice three different ideas or whatever, then come Sunday, Greg would be calling the plays he wanted, and you weren't always doing the same thing in the game that you were doing during the week. There seemed to be conflict within the coaching staff, with the front office. The players felt at the time like they weren't the players the coaches wanted."

Cheating

Golf at the Midlane Country Club in north suburban Wadsworth has been a Bears standard for years. And it has seen its share of hijinks.

A lot of the players took up golf and started playing at Midlane, which also meant that they weren't always very good. That didn't stop them from competing and doing anything within the rules—and beyond—to win.

In fact, creative cheating was sometimes in order and a goal in itself; what can you get away with? And with the stakes sometimes reaching into the hundreds of dollars per hole as the rounds wore on, players pushed the limits.

Glen Kozlowski was caught in the act once. Playing with Neal Anderson and Cap Boso, Koz hit one into the rough near a green. He was in amid some small trees and out of sight—or so he thought.

A member of the foursome, who shall remain anonymous, remembers: "I'm watching a ways off, waiting for Koz before I hit, and all I can see are his feet. All of a sudden a hand comes down, picks up the ball, then the club swoops down like a swing, and a little later the ball flips up onto the green.

"Koz comes out of the bushes: 'I couldn't see where it went; where'd it go?' Somebody said, 'Wow, it's up by the pin. Great shot.' I couldn't let Cap lose the hole on a hand mashie, so I told Cap and he goes flying across the green, Koz takes off laughing, and Cap catches him and they go wrestling all over the place, yelling. I don't know if we even finished the round, but that was golf with Koz."

Complete lie, says Koz.

"That's total bull!" Kozlowski rebuts. "He made that up. Harbs did that, not me!"

"See, what I did, I was in a place where I had no shot and yeah, I threw it out. Cap's yellin', 'You can't do that!' I said, 'Hey, I didn't have a shot. What was I supposed to do? And yeah, I threw it. But it was a great throw!'"

Speak Up

Cornerback Lemuel Stinson, asked if he intended to discuss his situation with the coaches, said, "We'll get together and conversate on things."

The White Guy

Tom Waddle took his share of knocks. Some had to do with the color of his skin. So did some of the compliments.

"Defensive backs all saw me as this slow little white guy and for some reason thought the way to play me was to beat the stuffing out of me at the line of scrimmage. So I probably saw more bump-and-run coverage than most guys.

"There were some overtly racist things, more in the early years until you earn people's respect. There were some things that weren't politically correct today. I can honestly say that I did not stoop to that level, although I did try to bite Benny Blades' finger off.

"I unfortunately crossed his path and Joey Browner's. Joey was six three, 235 and brought the hammer. Wasn't the friendliest guy. And Blades was just out there to hurt you.

"I was playing Deion Sanders, who was a great guy, in '91 or '92 and had five catches, 70-some yards and a touchdown on the day. After the game I'm feeling good about myself and here comes Deion Sanders up to me. He wasn't a mouthy guy, a classy guy who worked hard out there. He says, 'Waddle.'

"I said, 'Yes, Mr. Sanders?'

"'Waddle, you're the best white wide receiver I've ever played against,' Sanders said."

Waddle was flying high. But not for long.

"I go into the locker room feeling good, walk over to John Mangum, probably my best friend on the team, and he says, 'Great game. You had some catches, yards, you scored, and we got the win,'" Waddle recalls.

"I said, 'John, that's not even the best part.' I told him Deion had come up to me and told me I was the best white wide receiver he's played against.

Neal Anderson
AP/WWP

"He kind of looked at me, laughed, and in that Southern drawl of his, says, 'Well, let's see. There's you, Eddie McCaffrey and Ricky Proehl. Shoot, there's only three of you in the league.'"

Just a Little More Ming

McMichael provided his own form of rookie orientation for young Bears in 1986. The rookies were in a small room next to the locker room, away from the veterans. McMichael blasted open the door, stalked into the room and began pounding his head with his helmet.

Blood was coming down and McMichael was beating himself, bellowing, "You better be ready!" Then he stalked back out of the room.

No one spoke at first. The rooks looked around nervously at each other, until finally No. 1 pick Neal Anderson, in his Florida drawl, observed what they were all thinking: "Ah don' know what the hay-ell that means," Anderson said, "but that boy's a fool."

Players "Strike"

The Bears were affected like everyone else by the labor problems that cut into the 1982 and 1987 seasons, shortening them to nine and 15 games respectively. But the Bears staged a work stoppage of their own in 1991 as well.

The players were fed up with not having a decent indoor practice facility. When the weather was intolerable outside, they were forced to get on buses and ride to an area high school and use the gymnasium there, practicing in basketball shoes with full pads and on a basketball court.

When "practice" was over, it sometimes took two hours to bus back to Halas Hall in rush-hour traffic. That meant arriving occasionally as late as 7 p.m., still in pads, sweaty and still needing to shower and dress before going home at the end of a 13- to 14-hour day during the season.

"It really, whether they want to admit it, wore our team out," says defensive end Trace Armstrong.

So the players staged their "strike." They went out to practice fully dressed and ready to play. They went through stretching exercises, then as a group turned and walked off the field and back into the locker room at Halas Hall in Lake Forest.

Ditka, who had alienated himself from much of the team in 1987 by declaring that the strike-breaking players were "the real Bears," was furious. He and the other coaches tried to get into the locker room while the players were taking their stuff off, yelling that they needed to practice and get some work done.

Mike Singletary got up and stood outside the door and didn't move. "You guys," Singletary told the coaches, holding his ground, "shouldn't come in here right now."

They didn't.

Roomies

Guard Kurt Becker and receiver Glen Kozlowki were assigned as roommates. Bad pairing, for the room's sake.

Kozlowski was rehabbing an injured knee in 1986, had his leg in a cast and was talking to his wife on the phone. All of a sudden Becker jumped on his back and started pulling Koz's head back, demanding that Koz

Mike Singletary AP/WWP

tell his wife "Who's your daddy? Who's your daddy? Tell her who's your daddy."

Koz escaped, but the first stone had been cast. That night, while Becker slept, Koz wrapped blankets around Becker's feet and set them on fire. "Oh man," Koz marvels. "Those things went up like nothing I've ever seen. He's running around the room yellin' and screamin' and I thought he was going to die."

The next day, Becker snuck up behind his roomie and put him in a wrestler's sleeper hold and rendered Koz completely unconscious. But again, Becker had to sleep sometime, so Koz waited.

That night, after Becker'd finished the contents of a number of beverage bottles, Koz began firing the bottles against the cinderblock wall, just above Becker's head. Becker was comatose so he never woke up, until the next morning when he had to crawl out of bed over a bunch of broken glass and cut himself all up.

"Then [trainer] Freddie Caito comes around and makes us shake hands and promise to stop it," Koz says. "Too bad. We were having fun together. And hey, we were just getting started."

Clueless

Quarterback Jim Harbaugh lost his wallet in Glen Kozlowski's car. What was remarkable was that it had $1,200 in it. What was more remarkable was that Harbaugh didn't miss it for three weeks.

"I think I lost my wallet," Harbaugh told Kozlowski one day after practice.

"It wasn't that Harbs didn't miss $1,200," Koz says. "It was that he never went into his wallet so he didn't miss it. That's how clueless Harbs was."

Farewell

Pro football is a business. Players know it. Coaches know it. Fans know it. But when Mike Ditka left the Bears, "that was hard for me," recalls Tom Waddle. "When he left, for a lot of us, the wind kind of came out of the sails. The game had not become such a transient business and guys were still with their teams. So it was the passing of an era.

"And we weren't that bad a team. We weren't that bad. We just couldn't come through at the right times sometimes."

Hamp's Chronology

For most of the 1980s the Bears seemed invincible, and for much of it they were. But more went out of the team in the early successful seasons than many recognized.

"Every year's team's chemistry is different," Hall of Fame defensive lineman Dan Hampton says. "Into '84, we were still bulletproof and young. But by the time we'd won the Super Bowl, we'd shown a lot of age in two years. McMahon was more beat up, Walter was going from a guy averaging five a carry to three and a half, Covert's back was starting to go out, my legs, McMichael's knees...

"Going into the '86 season I told the guys on defense, 'We are going to have to be the ones that do it. Buddy's gone; we can't cry. And if we come in fourth or 10th or whatever on defense, everybody'll say it was Buddy Ryan.' So I wanted to make sure we all understood where we stood.

"In '87 we still had the nucleus of a good team, but it wasn't the same due to the fact that we practiced at such a clip, that we had such egos and pride, that we played every day hammer and tong. We didn't want to go 10-6 and just be good enough for the playoffs. In '86 we went 14-2. You do that and you're burning a lot of gas.

"By the '88 season, Otis was hurt and Wilbur was gone and we were playing with Rivera and Morrissey. Good solid players, but they didn't give us that great ability of Otis and Wilbur. Todd Bell wasn't the same, and Fridge had gained about 100 pounds and wasn't the same player.

"And Vince Tobin was not the same type of factor Buddy was. With Vince's ideology of more bend-don't-break, our defense wasn't as dangerous. In '84, '85, we were an 'offensive' defense. I always remember Bill Parcells and Chuck Noll telling me they had huge problems preparing for us.

"But by '87 we had slowed down enough to where we were almost blockable on occasion. In the 49er game, in the '88 championship, they were running one- and two-man patterns on us and staying in 'max-protection'. And you get two helmets on me and McMichael, with Richard out of the game, even with Singletary, we didn't have great players doing things. So our window of opportunity was shot.

"When Buddy left, Fridge went to 400 and became a non-factor after about '86. Certain players, if you don't challenge them, will take what they can get. I'm not dogging Fridge; I love Fridge. But by the middle of the '87 season he was nowhere near the player he was his rookie year. He had been a real solid player but now was getting knocked off the ball."

In 1987 the Bears were preparing to face the Raiders. Perry had not been playing especially well for a while, and the coaches made a change.

Tobin came in the meeting room and said, "Hampton, you're starting at right tackle."

McMichael and Hampton, who were more mobile than Perry and loved running stunts and games together, looked at each other.

"We had a good game, beat the Raiders 6-3, from that point on, it was me at defensive tackle, which really made for a better overall defense inside, with guys like Al Harris at left end and then Tyrone Keys. People don't always remember that in the '88 [NFC] championship game, the Niners just had Jerry Rice and John Taylor out on two-man patterns and the eight other guys in blocking for Montana.

"It was a great era, but like all good things, it started decaying from inside. It was a good run but kind of sad how it ended."

Chapter 4

1985

The 1985 Bears rank among the greatest teams, not only in franchise history, but also in the annals of NFL legend. The confluence of coaches, players and every other factor was like few others anywhere anytime, and there are untold events and stories behind the headlines.

Dallas Who?

The Dallas Cowboys were just so much road kill for the 1985 Bears, 44-0 losers to the Bears in a game that proved beyond any doubt that this was a team, if not for the ages, then certainly for the 1985 season.

Unfortunately, the Cowboys brought some of their fate on themselves.

"The first game of the year, we had to come from behind to win [against Tampa Bay]," says Dan Hampton. "Then we kind of got in synch and got going.

"But I will never forget getting ready for Dallas. Ditka was from Dallas and we'd played them a couple times and lost. We thought that if we don't do anything else, we need to win this game for Ditka. By then he had gotten to where we loved him. It took a year or two for us to understand. He's got a lot of bark on him and you have to figure him out.

"And by then we were ready to kick Dallas' ass. We're 11-0 and they're 8-3, and all week, Everson Walls is saying crap like, 'Yeah, the Bears are playing teams like Detroit and all these people. They haven't played anybody.' People pointed out that we're 11-0 and he's still, 'They haven't played anybody.'

"After we finish up with them and it's 44-0, a bunch of writers are around the locker, and I said, 'I have to give Everson Walls credit. He was right. We're 12-0 and we still ain't played nobody.'"

Priorities

Mike Tomczak had injured his right arm during a game and left Soldier Field with it in a sling, which was a problem when trying to navigate his truck. He was parked near the Mercedes Benz belonging to Steve McMichael and wife Debi. Not a good place to be with an injured arm.

McMichael had lined up a case of beers on his car trunk for some refreshment after the game. Tomczak, however, in trying to exit, bumped McMichael's Mercedes, sending the beers tumbling and rolling all over the parking lot.

McMichael immediately started trying to run down the rolling brew. Debi had a different worry, namely what had happened to the car.

"What are you doing?!" she screamed at McMichael.

The ever-pragmatic Texan kept gathering up the beers. "Baby," he drawled, "You can ALWAYS get another Mercedes."

Settle This

It was a fourth-and-one situation, a critical game moment, when linebacker Ron Rivera ran onto the field as a rookie in 1984. Up ahead of him were Dan Hampton and Steve McMichael in an intense discussion. Rivera hustled over to get in on the expertise the two veterans were obviously dispensing.

"Hey, Rivera, settle this," Hampton demanded. "Who's better: the blonde in section 22, row 7, or the brunette in 24, third row? I got $100 says the blonde."

"What do you say, rookie?" McMichael snarled.

Rivera knew enough to understand that he was in a world of hurt with either choice. Then came a flash of inspiration: "Hey, I like 'em both."

One answer, two enemies. On the way off the field after the defensive stop, he took shots from both, with the same line: "You idiot, you cost me $100."

Tough Change

Mike Hartenstine had been a successful defensive end for almost a decade when William Perry arrived as a draft choice. The defense was dominant, but Ditka wanted Perry to play, and Hartenstine lost his job even though he was outplaying Perry at the time.

"Ditka made him a media hero letting him run the ball and catch the ball," Hartenstine says. "I'm sitting there getting older. The media's loving Fridge and I'm outplaying the guy, but they had to play him, almost because of the media. Plus, they didn't want to look bad blowing a No. 1 pick.

"Ultimately Fridge was a good player and I liked him; it wasn't anything personal. I just hated that I lost my job in a situation where I shouldn't lose it. If I'm not out-producing somebody, then I should lose it.

"I played anywhere at that time, tackle or end. And we had that '46' where I'd always be that weak-side end because you had Wilbur and Otis flying in, so all you needed was back-side pickup. I was mostly on the right then."

Having been relegated to reserve status after laboring so many years to help his team get to the top made the Super Bowl just a little tainted.

"It was pretty bittersweet," Hartenstine says. "I felt a lot like Walter did. He didn't get a chance to score and I didn't get a chance to play against New England. We'd played them earlier when I was starting and beat 'em. I could've played the whole game and I wouldn't have hurt our defense. Richard got hurt one game and I played against Minnesota, which had one of the best offenses, and we shut them out. I knew I could play. Ditka did it, I'm sure, but Buddy was the one who told me."

Hampton remembers: "Halfway through the '85 season, Fridge had gotten in shape and was doing the offensive thing. And that was partly because Ditka didn't want to look like an idiot and Buddy's saying he's not good enough to play our defense.

"Hartenstine had been playing 11 years and was starting to slow down, so they decided, we're better with Fridge at tackle and Hampton at end because then we've got four young guys who can go."

Kicking: The Rough Life

"I didn't mind the kickers like Kevin Butler wearing the little shoulder pads and going around in the short-shorts," says linebacker Jim Morrissey.

"But what really got me was that when we went out to practice, Kevin and the kickers were putting on suntan lotion. I thought, yep, they're on a different schedule than we are."

Destroying the Giants

The game against the New York Giants in the '85 postseason was a signature game in a season full of them.

"The Giant game was big because we thought they were the second best team in football, and they would win it next year," says Dan Hampton. "We went with a real pass-defense type deal. They had a good offensive line, good back, good quarterback, and Buddy felt we had to be able to pressure Simms."

"He put me on the nose and basically just went with a five-man rush. Then we had all our games inside and they couldn't block us. The next deal was that we had played a good game the year before against Washington to get to the championship game, but then we stepped on our dicks. That was a big game. The Super Bowl was anticlimactic."

Shuffling

Not every player was on board for the legendary Super Bowl Shuffle.

"The biggest problem I had with the Super Bowl Shuffle was that they did it the day after the day we lost to the Dolphins," said Mike Hartenstine. "We're on the plane coming home from Miami and everybody's talking about going down to do the Super Bowl Shuffle. I was like, 'Screw you guys, we just lost a goddamn game and we're going to do a video about the Super Bowl after we got our asses handed to us. I'm not going down there.'

"To me it was just wrong. I probably would have done it if it was a different set of circumstances because it was a team kind of thing and I'm about the team. Actually I don't think Walter or McMahon did it that day. Hampton didn't do it, or McMichael. We were pissed."

Centers of Attention

The 1980s saw two of the best centers in NFL history playing at the same time: the Bears' Jay Hilgenberg and Miami's Dwight Stephenson.

"What Hilgy was so good at was letting you go the way you wanted, getting you off balance, and then dumping you," Dan Hampton remembers. "He was hardly ever on the ground.

"That's how Stephenson was. He took Fridge down a number of times in that Monday night game and everybody was thinking, 'Wow.' Fridge would go into him and Stephenson would just get that weight going and just throwing him on the ground. After the game

Buddy said, 'Here you are, 400 pounds, and the guy's throwing you around like a bag of shit.'"

Core of the 46

Few defenses in NFL history have terrorized the league the way the "46" defense of Buddy Ryan and the Bears did. But if the number-name of the defense recalled safety Doug Plank, the true flowering of the 46 came in '85, after Plank was gone.

"The whole thing was predicated on me," says Dan Hampton. "I could not get hooked either way and if I was just single-blocked, I had to hit the quarterback within two seconds. I don't mean to beat my drum, but it was the fact that I was un-blockable with a single block.

"It wasn't a lot of moves, more like a surge rush and hit the quarterback. It was predicated on us having three world-class pass rushers. It's just how are you going to handle it."

Buddy vs. Vince

The Bears' great defense of the 1980s arrived with Buddy Ryan, who was brought in from Minnesota by Neill Armstrong to be defensive coordinator. But Buddy wasn't the only defensive guru to direct that legendary defense.

Vince Tobin arrived in 1986 after Ryan left for the head-coaching job at Philadelphia. There were obvious differences from Ryan to Tobin, although the statistics actually improved under Tobin.

"Buddy had a great defensive philosophy and he wasn't afraid to use it," says Mike Hartenstine. "It was funny, because when Tobin came, he had as good a defense as Buddy did as far as what he could throw at you, but he would never use it.

"We could go in at halftime and Buddy would pull some defense that we hadn't run since the first day of training camp and we'd use it. Tobin'd say, 'Oh, they probably won't get it right.' If it wasn't in the game plan, he'd hesitate to use it. Buddy wouldn't."

The image that Tobin ran a taut ship and Ryan was the loose leader of a band of brigands wasn't completely accurate. Tobin was strict, sometimes to a fault, but Ryan had his lines of conduct and you'd better not cross them.

"Buddy was actually a real disciplinarian," said Hartenstine, who played for Jack Pardee, then Buddy, then Vince. "It seemed like he was real easy-going, but if you didn't do it exactly the way it was supposed to be done, you caught hell for it.

"We'd be out there running 'gassers' where you run goal line to the 20 and back, to the 30 and back, and everybody had to touch the line. We might be all the way from the goal line to the 50 and somebody's missed a line and he'd say, 'You're all doing it over.' So you didn't want to be the guy who missed the line, or the guy who let everybody else down. He was very smart, too.

"We'd argue and fight over tackles and sacks and finally Buddy'd say, 'OK, that's enough, let's get to work.' But when Tobin came in, you couldn't say a word in the meeting, you just had to sit there and listen to what he had to say. It was more of a team with Buddy. And we worked and knew when to work."

Dan Hampton remembers the first meeting with Tobin and the change from Ryan.

"Buddy had a very dominant personality," Hampton says. "The best players in the world could be belittled by Buddy and I wouldn't bat an eye. You would never back-talk him. Then Vince comes in and he doesn't have the credentials to tell us to get our feet off the chairs.

Buddy had an unorthodox way of doing things. Players would lie on the floor, watch film, and if they fell asleep, they fell asleep. As long as they got done what they needed for Sunday.

Ditka once happened by a meeting of the defensive unit and saw bodies on the floor.

"What are you doing, letting these guys lie on the floor, sleeping?" he demanded of Ryan.

"Yeah, and I hear 'em snoring sometimes too," Ryan shot back.

His Big Break

Linebacker Jim Morrissey was an 11th-round draft choice in 1985, another of those late-round draft choices that Jim Finks and the scouting staff seemed to find that were part of the unsung foundation of a dynasty. But for Morrissey, it took a little help in the form of holdouts by Al Harris and Todd Bell in the Super Bowl season.

"I came in in 1985 but was released on the last cut of training camp and went back to my hometown of Flint, Mich.," Morrissey says. "I got a call from Bill Tobin the next week, after the Bears had beaten Tampa Bay in the opener. Brian Cabral was a linebacker for the Bears and hurt his knee on a kickoff, so the Bears called me back and signed me for a week-to-week situation.

"At that time Todd Bell and Al Harris were sitting out the '85 season, and Coach Ditka, who was always fair, said, 'I don't care how big you are; I don't care how fast you are or slow, or what you look like in the shower. If you're a football player, you can play on my football team,' and that's what I wanted to hear as an 11th-round draft pick.

"When I came in he said, 'I need you for special teams; I don't need you for playing linebacker. You're week to week, so enjoy yourself. If either Todd or Al come back, you're the odd man out, unfortunately.' So I went week to week living with my grandparents in Northbrook and had a great time."

"What he doesn't tell you," guard Tom Thayer joked at the 2003 Fan Convention, "is that he disconnected the phones of both Todd Bell and Al Harris the whole year."

"Don't tell Todd or Al that," Morrissey said.

Buddy On Motivation

Mike Ditka may have been cast as the master motivator, but few did it with the style of Buddy Ryan.

"We're watching film one week and there's O. J. Anderson running over somebody," Dan Hampton remembers. "Ryan says to Otis, 'Ooh, you better get hurt in practice this week. I don't want him running over you like that.'

"That's all he had to say. Otis was ready to go, muttering 'I'll show that *#*$&%&%.' And he was talking about showing Buddy, not just Anderson.

"He'd tell McMichael, 'McMichael, I don't care if you go out and get drunk. Just don't take any of the 'real' players with you.' And he'd say it in a way that would have McMichael just fuming.

"Vince didn't have the personality to do that. Vince was more of just telling you when to show up, what to do and you did it."

Ryan had an impact on the offense. "He'd see that McMahon was our best chance, so rather than yell at him because he wasn't like Terry Bradshaw, Buddy would be looking at him, finding ways to pump him up," Hampton says. "And he did that to the whole team.

"He'd say to the offensive line, 'You fat asses can't block anybody in practice; how you going to do it in a game?' And Covert, Bortz and those guys would turn into animals."

A Case of Respect

For the Ditka Bears, there was no half-speed in practice. It was all or nothing. But there was a bond even between combatants.

"There was a great respect," says Dan Hampton. "Our defensive line could all go in and pick up 300 pounds, do reps with it and power-clean. The reason we were so good was because we had explosion. And those offensive guys were the same. Covert was a bad-ass. Bortz, you'd have to kill him if you got in a fight with him."

Meal Ticket

As a group, the defensive linemen were always different. They came in and as a unit decided they wanted to have hot lunches. They spread it around and a couple times a week somebody bought hot lunches. Pretty soon the offensive guys were sitting there eating their baloney sandwiches and the defense was having hot lunches, and the offensive guys started grousing about it. Management got upset at the whining and got hot lunches for everybody.

CHAPTER 5

EARLY DA COACH

Making Changes

After George Halas hired Mike Ditka to coach the Bears, changes followed immediately. Some in fact seemed even sooner.

When Ditka took over the Bears, it was with the idea that he would make changes. Part of that would include weeding out players he didn't think fit with the program.

"It was brutal for everybody," said Mike Hartenstine. "He came in and we met up at a bar called Me and Mrs. P's. Ditka's up there with his wife, me and my wife, Hamp and his wife, Steve and his wife.

"Ditka buys every bottle of champagne in the place and we drink it all, the eight of us. Ditka's getting all looped up and starting to go, 'I'm getting rid of this guy, he ain't shit' and 'This guy's no good' and these are guys we've played with for years, our buddies, and we didn't want to hear this. 'This guy's worthless.' And this is before we even had a practice together!

"I'm sitting there thinking, man, I don't know if I want to know all this stuff. I might be on the list too."

Nicknaming

How did Steve McMichael get his other nickname of Mongo? From the character played by Alex Karras in the film *Blazing Saddles*, in which Karras gave his signature performance, knocking a horse unconscious with a roundhouse right.

And when did James Thornton become "Robocop?" Television commentator John Madden observed that Thornton had the same physique as the half-man, half-robot character in the movie *Robocop*.

Still More Ming

In 1983 the Washington Redskins put a 24-7 thrashing on the Bears, after which coach Mike Ditka was in a foul mood in the locker room. But no one could find McMichael.

All of a sudden the door burst open and in came Ming the Merciless, who reduced the room to laughter.

"Quick, lock the doors," he roared. "The Redskins are coming in here after us to kick our asses some more."

First Impressions

Hall of Fame defender Dan Hampton had arrived in 1979, the fourth overall pick of the draft, and liked previous coach Neill Armstrong. But the team was slipping in the wrong direction.

"In 1981 we're getting ready to play the final game of the season," Hampton says. "Ricky Watts was drinking Drambuie before the game to warm up. Dan Neal came to me and said, 'Guys are drinking over here, go say something to them.'

"I said, 'Go tell the damn coaches.' They went and told the coaches and one of the coaches came to me and said, 'Go tell them to stop.' The inmates were running the asylum. That's something we never had a problem with with Ditka. We didn't have a good team at first for a year or two, but we knew we were pointed in the right direction.

"He showed up with a Bible and George Halas and had this competitive fire inside him. Buddy had a condescending attitude toward him. Buddy was an old-school guy who said you became a coordinator first, had success and then become a head coach. He thought Ditka had kind of back-doored the thing. It took a while for Mike to earn respect.

"Buddy told him to put Mark Bortz on offense. By '84, it wasn't the same garden-variety offensive player. Ditka was getting guys who had something.

"It's one of those deals where he wasn't happy and was going to make changes. That made us ecstatic. We liked the guys on the team, but we wanted to win, and if we had to get new players to do it, so be it. He thought like we did, that we had to get to where we could whip Pittsburgh's ass, or match up with Dallas. He said, 'My goal is to win a Super Bowl. I won a championship as a player, as an assistant coach, and I know what we have to do to win one.' That was like pie in the sky to us because we'd always been middle of the pack.

"In 1983 we went up to Minnesota and beat the Vikings. Ozzie [Jim Osborne] had tears in his eyes after the game and I said, 'What's the matter?' He said, 'I've been here 11 years and we've never beaten Minnesota up here.' I said to myself, 'Shit, it's changing. We're not doormats any more.'"

Nice Guys Don't Finish

Bob Thomas finished his Chicago career about the time Ditka's coaching reign was beginning. It didn't take long for Da Coach to make an impression on the veteran kicker.

"At the end of my career I was playing for Ditka and we were playing the Detroit Lions," Thomas says. "Eddie Murray was the kicker for the Lions then and Ditka sent Dave Duerson after Eddie towards the end of the game, and of course he killed Eddie.

"I never thought it was a good idea to do that, by the way. Teams had a tendency to remember that sort of thing and retaliate the next time they saw you.

"So Eddie's down on the field, the game was stopped and after the game, Gary Fencik and I, who had played golf with Eddie and he was somewhat of a friend, went over into the tunnel to see how he was doing. He thought he'd separated his shoulder, so it was bad.

"The next day, Monday, WGN radio always used to have a call-in show with Ditka and Wally Phillips. And we would all listen religiously Monday morning. Ditka says, 'You know what's wrong with this team? It's not like the old days. We have a bunch of wussies on this team that go over and apologize to people on the other sideline.'

"And I'm thinking, 'Oh no, holy crap.' So I pick up the *Tribune* and it says a couple of players apologized to Eddie Murray and I'm thinking, OK, at least I'm not named. Then I remembered that there was another paper in town, so I pick up the *Sun-Times* and there it is: Bob Thomas and Gary Fencik 'apologizing' to Eddie Murray.

"So I walk into the locker room and Fencik is sitting there in his locker. I say, 'Hey, did you listen to Wally Phillips this morning?' He said, 'Yeah, at least it's not in the *Trib*.' I said, 'You wanna see the *Sun-Times*?'

"He turns white as a sheet and I, being a lawyer, say we're going to go up there and we are going to cop a plea and do whatever we can to get out of this. We go up to the office and Iron Mike is sitting there, smoking a cigar, and we say to him, 'Mike, it really wasn't an apology. We really just wanted to see how the guy was. We play golf with him in the off season, he's been a friend,' and so forth. Fine.

"We leave and we're relieved, thinking, 'OK, he took that pretty well.' So we head down to the team meeting, and in comes Ditka. He goes off: 'You know why we're losing? We have wussie players like Thomas and Fencik.'

"So I guess things weren't completely fine."

Getting Offensive

"The thing I loved about Ditka," says Mike Hartenstine, "was that I'd been with two defensive-minded coaches in Pardee and Neill, and Ditka was the first offensive-minded coach for me. And that's what I always thought we needed, because our defense never seemed to be the problem. It wasn't just his presentation that 'I'm here, we're going to win the Super Bowl.' Just that he came in and said, 'This is my offense.'

"Trouble was, he came in with the Dallas offense, all that motion and crap. And we couldn't do it. So he said, OK, now THIS is my offense. And he came up with something else. I thought that was great. Just put points on the board."

CHAPTER 6

THE "BETWEEN YEARS"

After George Halas stepped down following his fourth stint as head coach, the franchise slumped at first, then had some up-and-down times under coaches Jim Dooley, Abe Gibron, Jack Pardee and Neill Armstrong. There were a couple of trips to the playoffs, but it was mostly a time of winning battles (the Bears were a team few wanted to play despite Chicago being among the NFL doormats) and losing wars. These were the Between Years, between Halas and Ditka, and they have their own stories and tales.

Jumping Ship

The Bears struggled through the early 1970s before Jack Pardee arrived and the Bears made the playoffs in 1977 with the coming of age of the '75 draft that included Bob Avellini, Walter Payton, Roland Harper, Mike Hartenstine, Tom Hicks, Virgil Livers, Doug Plank and Revie Sorey. But the satisfaction was short-lived when Pardee abruptly left to coach the Washington Redskins after giving his Bears short shrift before meeting the Dallas Cowboys in the playoffs.

"Pardee kind of jumped ship on us bad and I never appreciated that, ever," defensive end Hartenstine says. "It came down to the understanding that he was going to get the Washington job if he got us into the playoffs, and he got us into the playoffs in '77. We were getting ready to play Dallas in the wild card game and it's something like 60-below here, and Pardee says, 'No, I want you guys here, in Chicago, because the holidays are coming up and I want you to be with your families.'

"Well, that was all bullshit. Pardee was packing his house up, getting ready to move, so he didn't want to take us anywhere because he was trying to get packed up, get his kids into schools, and get the move going. So he kept us here instead of going somewhere warm to prepare for Dallas, like you normally would for a playoff game. Everybody did after that.

"It was so cold that you couldn't be outside for more than 45 minutes at a time. You couldn't work on anything offensively timing-wise because everything was ice and frozen and you couldn't win. I was disappointed because he never gave us a shot in that game.

"We ended up getting blown out in Dallas and I hated that he wanted us here just because he wanted to take care of his house. And we knew it at the time. He was offering [Doug] Buffone the house if he wanted to buy it, so we all knew he was going."

Blasted

"You think kickers never get hit, but teams always send some big guy after the kicker almost every play," says Bob Thomas. "Usually you can get around them, but one time against Green Bay I'm running down, feeling happy about the kickoff, and one of these linemen was a little irritated that I'd faked him out.

"As the back started down the sideline, I turned, never saw this guy and got hit. I really looked on film like a crash dummy in one of those seat-belt commercials. Jack Pardee was our coach and showed that play in slow motion about 20 times. After that he gave me a bottle of wine for coming of age as a football player.

"I went to the sideline and wailed, 'Does that happen to people on every play?'"

Sticking to Basics

Bears coaches have long been criticized for conservatism, which might have stemmed from having a long history of being supplied with great running backs. Whatever the reason, there was definitely some resistance to change.

"I came into the league in '75 and we really weren't a very potent team but we had a lot of good people," Mike Hartenstine says. "And we played people hard, really got after people. Teams didn't usually win the week after they played us. In those days you could really grow a team too. I loved playing with those guys. Even though we were 4-10 my rookie year, we were almost never out of games.

"We had Pardee as our head coach and he was obviously a great defensive coach, but offensively he was a lot of five yards and a cloud of dust. When Walter ran for 275 yards, we won 10-7, which was ridiculous. Sid Gillman came in and tried to help the offense out, but Pardee wouldn't listen to anything he would say, so Sid left after one year, 1977.

"Bob Avellini was totally a Sid freak, loved Sid and wanted to throw the ball because he knew that when you had a great runner you could throw the ball because everybody was going to be up there to stop Walter. Pardee said no, we were going to run the ball."

Heavy Lifting

"I used to love working out with Plank," Mike Hartenstine says. "He was a great guy to lift weights, coming up with new ideas to do things and tax ourselves. One time, though, we were lifting weights and all of a sudden, Plank's finger just exploded. Exploded. Blood all over the place."

Get Out of the Way!

Bob Thomas was the Bears' place-kicker for many years, but he almost didn't survive his rookie preseason.

"I was drafted by the Rams, cut in the last cut, and re-signed by the Rams," Thomas says. "I had to go through procedural waivers, and the Redskins and Bears picked me up. Because the Bears were lower in the standings, I ended up with Chicago.

"My roommate was a guy named Doug Plank. When I walked in, I knew he was the right guy to ask. I asked him, 'Doug, what happens if I have to make a tackle?' I don't want you to think I didn't make any tackles at Notre Dame, but we were playing Northwestern at the time.

"Doug said, 'Bob, they're going to see you're a little guy, see that No. 16 and that you're wearing black shoes where everybody else is wearing white. So just plant your feet and when they try to run around you, make the tackle and you'll be a hero.

"I had no cause to use that information my rookie year until the last game. We were playing the New Orleans Saints and winning. I kick off the last time of the year and here comes this running back, six-two, 235 pounds, down the sidelines, and there is nobody between him and the goal line except me.

"A lot of things went through my mind, like my Mom would be crying at the funeral. But I thought I had to at least make an attempt at what Plank had said. So I planted my feet firmly in front of that back, and when it was all done, I had cleat marks up one side of me and down the other.

"The only reason he didn't score was that he tripped over my goofy facemask when he stepped on my face. Plank was laughing and said, 'Bob, that's the one guy I wasn't counting on.'"

The Sack

Mike Hartenstine's sack of Philadelphia Eagles quarterback Ron Jaworski in 1980 was one of the highlight-film hits in Bears history. What happened after the hit, though, was as much a tale as the sack itself.

"Jaworski just held the ball too long," Hartenstine says. "I was blocked on the play going against Stan Walters and took a big outside rush, and I'm rushing, rushing, rushing, and I get around Walters, and

Jaworski's a little ways away. He's holding the ball, holding the ball, holding the ball, and I'm running at him and figured I'd never get there.

"Well, I whacked him. There was no penalty on the play. He went out of the game for a couple plays but he came back.

"I got in the locker room and all the reporters are asking, 'What do you think about Vermeil wanting the league to fine you for that?' I said, 'Fine me for what?' 'He said you speared Jaworski, tried to kill his quarterback.' I didn't know how he could say that because there wasn't even a flag on it.

"A week later I get a letter from the NFL that I'm being fined $1,000 for spearing. So my agent and I go to New York to appeal it. I'm sitting there with Rozelle and we're looking at the thing from every angle, all over the place, and he's got all his henchmen there and they're cringing every time they show the hit. Everybody keeps saying, 'You speared him, you speared him.'

"Finally I said, 'You know, we've got Cs on our helmet. If I speared him with my head down, that C would be facing down pointing at the ground. When I hit him, you could see the C still up. My head's not down.

"Then Rozelle says, 'Yeah, you're right, you didn't spear him. But you hit him too vigorously, so we're keeping your money.' So I won the appeal but I still lost my money. I didn't win anything except to know that I was right and I didn't spear him.

"The thing was, the next time we played them, I speared him right in the sternum. Definitely with my head down. He drops the ball, goes down, and McMichael picks it up, runs it to the 10 and we eventually score the touchdown.

"As I'm coming off the field, Fencik's looking at me, just patting the top of his helmet and smiling. I just smiled back and said, 'Yep, speared him that time, so I got my money's worth.'"

When the Light Came On

Every NFL player was good in college. But most don't have the talent, mind or some ingredient to make it at the next level. And even for the greatest, there was that moment of breakthrough when they start to figure it out.

"When I got here, everybody up here was physically as good as you are," says Dan Hampton. "I didn't have any technique. At Arkansas we were in pretty much a 'run' conference. I was terrific against the run but on pass rushes, I'd just run into the guy and try to rassle him and try to get off him. I wasn't getting to the quarterback.

"We were getting ready to play Tampa Bay in the fourth game of the season. Wednesday we were in meetings and Jerry Eckwood, who was with me at Arkansas, was running and was a great talent. They'd pitch the ball to him and he'd sweep, outrun everybody and gain 20 yards.

"Buddy says to me, 'Big Rook, this kid from Arkansas, has he got great speed?' I said something like,

'Supposedly he ran a 4.3 in the combine.' Gary Fencik was in the back of the room and said, 'Yeah, and supposedly you was a great pass rusher.' Everybody laughed, but boy, that pissed me off.

"Later that day I was downstairs watching film and heard someone in another room, and I stuck my head in. It was Ted Albrecht. He was watching film on Leroy Selmon. He was always a big film guy. I asked him if that was Leroy, and he said, 'Yeah, he's the best I play against.' So I came in, sat down and started watching.

"I noticed that everything he did was keeping someone off balance. That's basically it. When you're playing basketball and you're trying to get to the basket, you're keeping the defensive guy off balance. It's the same thing, getting people off balance and getting rid of them.

"That game I had two sacks. It was just like the light went on watching Leroy and emulating what he did. It was incredible. All this was possible. At the end of my rookie year, Buddy Ryan told me I was playing as well as any defensive lineman in the game. The next year I made All-Pro."

The light had come on.

Point of Pride

Mike Hartenstine rarely missed a play in his career, let alone a game. Sometimes that required some creativity as well as a high tolerance for pain.

"I enjoyed that I never missed a game," Hartenstine says. "I missed one game in my career. I missed a high school game. None in junior high, one in high school, none in college, none in the pros through 11 years. I had two separated shoulders at the same time and once sprained both feet and that was hard. But you just do it.

"When I broke my thumb I had two pins sticking out of my thumb and it was pretty painful. The doc just taped it up and I think I had one of my better games, against Minnesota.

"But after it was fixed, the pins were sticking out and they put a cast right over the pins. So every time I would hit somebody, it would drive the pins in. I said, this isn't going to work, and had the doc cut a hole in the cast right over the pins, and I concocted this plastic bubble over it and that made it a lot easier."

Brian's Tune

Ed McCaskey took care of the family of Brian Piccolo when Brian was fighting his losing battle with cancer. He went to see Piccolo one last time and broke down when he saw how ravaged Piccolo was by the disease.

Piccolo saw Ed's tears and reassured him. "Don't worry, Big Ed," Piccolo said. "I'm not afraid of anything—only Nitschke."

Piccolo died the next day.

Good-Hands Guy

Kickers never had it too rough in training camp. Sometimes, though, there was a little pain to be endured.

"It was always tough for me in training camp because the toughest thing we had to do was play catch with the quarterbacks," says Bob Thomas. "There were usually three quarterbacks. My first year was Bobby Douglass' last year, and I noticed that the other two quarterbacks paired up really quick, and told me I was going to warm up Bobby Douglass. And he threw the ball about 150 miles an hour, knocked me down a few times.

"I wasn't happy to see Bobby go, but at least I wouldn't have to play catch with him. And then they drafted Vince Evans."

Tough Guys

Wally Chambers, a first-round draft choice of the Bears, was one of the dominant defensive linemen of his day. But few knew the whole story about how tough he really was.

"Wally was really awesome," says Mike Hartenstine. "The funny thing about Wally was that he had such great ability, strong and quick, but we'd be at practice and Wally would never practice. I'd wonder what was up with Wally because I had to do my stuff and then do some of his stuff, which was twice the work.

"I asked what the deal was and they said, 'Oh, Wally's got gout.' I couldn't understand that. Then later in my life I started getting gout attacks and I don't know how the guy could even play. I couldn't imagine playing with it. But he would play games and be effective in games. It was so painful.

"But Wally did and played well. That made him even more amazing."

Playing alongside Chambers and others who followed was Jim Osborne, a character in his own right. "Ozzie was a funny guy. We were playing down in Atlanta and running down a play, and Hamp just pushes Ozzie so Hamp could get to the play. Ozzie goes down and all of a sudden you hear this shriek and screaming. He'd hit a sprinkler head, cut his knee open and he's bleeding all over the place, screaming like a banshee."

Halas Linguistics

"When I arrived," Bobby Douglass remembers, "Mr. Halas had just quit coaching and Jim Dooley was my coach. But Mr. Halas was ever-present. We'd have quarterback meetings every day and he would bring me into his office and we'd get into a cussing match pretty much every day.

"I learned more words from him than I did in any of the training camps."

With Friends Like That, Who Needs Enemies?

Mike Hartenstine came into the NFL when linebacker Doug Buffone was an established veteran. Buffone helped Hartenstine learn the NFL, including when to duck.

"Douggie taught me so much," Hartenstine says. "I hear him on the radio sometimes saying that I helped him stay on, but he really helped me. I was pretty good at two-gapping and keeping guys off Doug, and he knew I would be going where I had to go. I think we didn't give up two yards a run to our side, more like 1.6 yards or something like that.

"But I remember that he knocked me out in the Astrodome against Houston. He was swinging around the quarterback and kicked me right in the head. I was out. I was out twice in my career and that was a pretty good one."

CHAPTER 7

'63 CHAMPIONS AND THE SIXTIES

The sixties were among the most tumultuous times in American history, so it's only fitting perhaps that they rank among the most turbulent in Bears history as well. From the peak of the 1963 NFL championship to the valley of the 1-13 season of 1969, it was a time of extremes: Dick Butkus, Gale Sayers, Doug Atkins and dozens of others who were as colorful as the time in which they lived and played.

The Pick

The winning touchdown in the championship game was set up by an interception from defensive end Ed O'Bradovich, who sniffed out a pass headed for the Giants' right flat.

"We had it nailed down," O'Bradovich says. "Joe Fortunato knew exactly where and when they were going to do it. On that particular play, Joe called it, 'Watch out for the screen,' just to remind me. Stroud was the offensive tackle and he starts dropping back, but he was too good. I wasn't going to suck in on it.

"So I went just so far in, then broke out into the flat, and next damn thing I know, the ball's coming and I put my left hand up and brought it in. I went a few yards and it turned out to be the winning points in the world championship game.

"The goofy part was, Y. A. Tittle after that game was on the front page of *Sports Illustrated*, all messed up, blood on his uniform, and that uniform winds up in the Hall of Fame. And we won the damn game."

Getting Along

Offensive and defensive players don't necessarily dislike each other, but sometimes there's tension when one unit isn't holding up its end of things. The '63 Bears were a legendary defensive unit, but offense was another matter.

During one dry spell for the offense, as the two units passed each other with the defense leaving the field after getting the ball on a turnover, expectations were spelled out.

"Just hold 'em," defensive end Ed O'Bradovich snarled at the offensive players. "Just give us a rest, get a first down or two, and we'll come back and get you six. Don't fuck it up."

The guys on offense had their own perspective on that rift.

"That stuff was mostly from the defensive team," said quarterback Bill Wade. "The offense never paid much attention to all that. The defensive team just seemed to need something to gear itself up. We were out there just to do the job. We gave people a lot of fits offensively. Even though we averaged 14 points a game, our turnover ratio was the smallest in the league.

"Offensively we thought we did our part and they did their part. They were more colorful, you might say."

Violent World

New York Giants middle linebacker Sam Huff became a national celebrity when he was wired for sound and filmed during a game. The show, "The Violent World of Sam Huff," was an eye-opener to the NFL game, letting people see inside the game as never before.

But Huff wasn't necessarily the legend around the NFL that the publicity factory of the New York media made him. Huff would go on to make the Hall of Fame, but don't sell "Sam Huff the Legend" to the Bears. They regularly faced true Hall of Fame middle linebackers like Green Bay's Ray Nitschke and Detroit's Joe Schmidt, besides having the originator of the middle linebacker, Hall of Famer Bill George.

Sports Illustrated came to George, who was one of the premier middle linebackers himself, and interviewed George about what he thought of the notion of wiring up Huff for a TV special. George thought for a second and suggested a casting change.

"If they're really going to do it right," George muttered, "they oughtta get Joe Schmidt to play the part of Huff."

I'll Get You

Ed O'Bradovich was one of the toughest members of a tough defense. He didn't ask any quarter, nor did he give any. But there was a code among warriors, and woe to the enemy who violated that. New York Giants running back Phil King found that out when he hit Eddie O. from behind after a play in the Bears-Giants game in 1962.

"We're playing in Wrigley Field and a play is over with and I'm standing there," O'Bradovich recalled. "All of a sudden something hits me, BAM, from behind, and I'm flying through the air. I get my senses, turn around, and I see this No. 24, who turns out to be King, and he starts running.

"I take out after him and he runs behind a bunch of Giants and I'm trying to grab him, swinging at everything, which is stupid because all you do is break your hand. There was no flag and nobody knew, so everybody's screaming at me, 'What are you doin'?! You're losing the game for us!' So Don Chandler kicks a field goal and they beat us. Man, I was feeling bad, young guy playing with all those great veterans.

"I was thrown out of the game, but in those days you didn't have to leave the sidelines. So I was looking at him and pointing at him, 'You son of a bitch, I'm going to get you.' It's getting down toward the end of the game, and he's got his eye on me, I got my eye on him.

"Bang, the gun goes off, and he takes off running for the dugout. I take off from our bench sprinting after the guy. Down in the dugout all the Giants are there waiting for him and it was an ugly scene. I went down into the dugout and finally I said, 'You tell that son of a bitch, he's gotta come out of Wrigley Field sooner or later and I'm going to be waiting by the bus for him.' But he dodged me and I never got him back.

"That was Sunday and we had Monday off. Tuesday I get there, get dressed, waiting to have our meeting, and somebody walks down and says, 'The Old Man wants to see you.' I'm thinking, 'Oh brother, here we go.' I went upstairs and Halas says, 'Sit down, kid.' Here I am, starting as a rookie and he says to me, 'Kid, I don't want you to ever forget this. You lost the game for us. They fined you $100. So you know what I'm going to do? I'm going to fine you another $100. So have a nice day.' That was Halas.

"Then I ran into Phil King at the Muelbach Hotel. We're touring with the Harlem Globetrotters all over the country, and we're in Kansas City. King was at the hotel and somebody comes up and says, 'He knows you're here and he's hiding.' I couldn't find the son of a bitch."

"Big Man"

Doug Atkins in his prime, and probably for a while after that, was the most feared man in the National Football League. There have been others who were feared but few as colorful to that point that everywhere players meet, there are Doug stories.

Atkins was huge, six foot eight, 260 pounds, and athletic. He played in the era before sacks were counted, but he and Deacon Jones, the man who coined and popularized the term "sack," were the greatest of their day.

Big Man, as Atkins' teammates addressed him, was just as interested in running up impressive totals off the field. He and defensive tackle Fred Williams both loved martinis, so one day Fred challenged Atkins to a contest.

They went out after practice to see who could drink the most, last man standing wins. The players knew the two were holding their drink-off and came in the next morning to find Atkins and Williams present, mostly, but looking like road kill. They asked Williams what had happened.

"Well, Doug had 21 and I had 21," Williams reported.

"So it was a tie?" Ed O'Bradovich quizzed.

"No," Williams said, "I figure Doug won because he threw me over his shoulder and carried me home."

Equipment Games

The Bears were in training camp at St. Joe's in Renssalaer, Ind., and everyone went out for a few pops the night before the start of practices. The next morning, about 9 a.m., the players were dressing, going to their meetings and starting to do warmup exercises. No Doug.

Halas gave his welcome-to-camp speech and went to his golf cart as players headed for their drills. Still no Doug.

Then out from the locker room came Atkins. Just dressed in shorts, a helmet with no facemask, no shirt. He ran slowly past the Old Man in his golf cart without either of them uttering a word. The players were all watching as Atkins jogged along the Christmas tree line by the field, then walked along a road, then trotted around the whole perimeter of the field as Halas just watched, not saying a word.

Doug ran right past Halas again and headed straight into the clubhouse. No practice. After practice the players headed into the lunch room and there was Atkins going through the lunch line.

"Hey, Big Man, what the hell was that?" he was asked.

"I's just breaking in my new helmet," Atkins drawled and went back to eating his lunch.

OK, Doug. No further questions.

Mike Ditka as a player. ***AP/WWP***

Welcome to the NFL, Rook

During Mike Ditka's rookie season, he went against Baltimore linebacker Bill Pellington, a renowned tough guy with a reputation. On the game's first play, Pellington punched Ditka squarely in the mouth. Not to be outdone, Ditka did exactly the same thing to Pellington on the next play.

Things went on like that for a while. Finally Ditka felt something land on his arm: a piece of cloth with a lead ball tied up in it. Ditka thought Pellington was now trying to get him with a blackjack and went to the referee with his complaint.

"Give me that damn thing," the official barked. "That's my flag!"

Outta Chicago

Halas and the Bears were the first team to lose a player to the rival American Football League when end Willard Dewveal played out his option in 1960 and signed with the Houston Oilers. They also could have lost Ditka.

In May, 1966 Ditka was offered a $50,000 bonus, $300,000 for three years and a home on a golf course to sign and play for Houston in 1967, when his Bears contract would be expired. It looked pretty good to someone making $25,000.

Ditka never played for the Oilers. The NFL and AFL worked out a merger plan that ended personnel raids. Still, Halas knew Ditka had signed with the rival league and the Bears exercised their option of cutting Ditka's salary 10 percent. Ditka exercised his right of free speech, more or less, and commented that Halas threw nickels around like manhole covers.

Ditka was traded to Philadelphia for quarterback Jack Concannon.

No Darts

Riley Matson and Ed O'Bradovich went out drinking one night in Renssalaer, came back in, and went to see if Doug Atkins was in, which wasn't likely. Atkins was in his room playing darts. O'Bradovich wanted to play.

"Let me play darts," O'Bradovich announced and grabbed the darts.

"No, you're not playing with my darts," Atkins declared, whereupon Big Man picked O'Bradovich up completely overhead and threw him down on the floor like a sack of potatoes.

"That was it for the darts," O'Bradovich recalls. "I learned damn quick right there. Don't interrupt the Big Fella when he's playing his darts."

Know What You're In For

"When you came to play the Bears it was very simple," said safety Davey Whitsell. "When you had to go up against guys like Doug Atkins, Stan Jones, Ed O'Bradovich, Bill George, Rich Petitbon, Larry Morris, you have some of those gorillas looking at you, come hell or high water, the Bears were going to put a physical beating on you.

"I don't care whether you won or lost. You were going to know you were in the damnedest game you were ever in in your whole life."

Smart Guy

Bill George invented the middle linebacker position when, as a nose tackle in a five-man line, he stood upright and a little back off the ball. Johnny Unitas once said that the only man he feared defensively was Bill George. Not for George's physical skills, which were enormous. But for his savvy.

"I'd be playing left defensive end and we might be on the goal line and I'd have outside containment," Ed O'Bradovich said. "Unitas would be calling an audible and George'd be yelling, 'O'B, O'B, jump inside, jump inside, they're coming inside.'

"Sure as shit, I'd jump inside the tackle or tight end and make the tackle and look great. He did that all the time. He could think right with Unitas."

Good and They Knew It

"We were completely loose in '63," said Doug Atkins. "We were loose the whole year. We laughed at everybody, and how we won, I don't know. We got every break going. We held the opposition to about 10 points."

Drinking Buddies

Defensive linemen Fred Williams and Doug Atkins had their share of epic drinking contests that usually ended with Atkins the winner. But not always.

"We got into a martini-drinking contest one night and I think it was 21 when I left it," Williams said. "He had to drive me home and how we made it I'll never know. My wife was in our apartment in Chicago, and when I got into the apartment, I fell into the bathtub and I couldn't get out.

"So she called Doug, who was living in the same apartment hotel. Doug comes down and she hands him the baby and says, 'You hold the baby, Doug,' but then she looks at him and says, 'Hell, you're as drunk as he is.'"

There'll Never Be Another Sayers

Gale Sayers came to the Bears one pick after Dick Butkus in the 1965 draft and became one of the greatest runners in NFL history in just 68 games. His career was shortened by a disastrous knee injury against the San Francisco 49ers in 1968, but his legend is vivid in the minds of those who tried to stop him, usually unsuccessfully.

"He was the only guy I think who could be running full speed, stop on a dime, tell you whether it's heads or tails, and not even break stride," said Hall of Fame Green Bay defensive back Herb Adderley.

Philadelphia Eagles defensive tackle Floyd Peters got credit for a tackle that he had very little to do with, all a credit to Sayers.

"He gave me a [shaking] fake and my body went one way, my mind went the other way and something happens to your motor when that happens," Peters said. "It's hard to explain. But my legs just went limp and I had nothing left.

"The only problem was, Gale made one too many fakes and came back into me. I hit him and knocked him down and he said, 'Nice tackle, Floyd.' I told him, 'I didn't tackle you. You ran into me.'"

Sayers didn't just seem to have eyes in the back of his head; he actually might have had them.

"I had great peripheral vision, there's no doubt about that," Sayers said. "I could see everybody on the field.

So I knew where to run or cut. I had a feel for where people were. I know that many times, many runs, I would watch the film and there'd be a fellow coming from my blind side. No way I could see him but I could feel him."

After the knee injury, Sayers returned the following season to rush for more than 1,000 yards, a further testament to his greatness. But the magic was gone and so was he a short time later, but not before he'd made his statement.

"They say that once you get a knee injury, you should think about quitting," Sayers said. "A running back very rarely comes back from the type of knee injury I had.

"But I wanted to prove that one could come back from a serious injury within a year. So many times they say it takes two years, three, but I wanted to prove that you could come back. And I had one of the worst knee injuries ever."

Weighty Matters

Rick Casares, one of the top running backs in Bears history, came to the Bears from Florida by way of the U.S. Army. The result was some exceptional conditioning, but it still didn't save him from Halas.

"In the off season, guys had to work other jobs so it was hard to get all the way in shape," Casares said. "When we came in you had to run the mile the first day in camp and there was a specific time that the

Gale Sayers *AP/WWP*

linemen had to make and one for the backs. You had to run before you got to camp, otherwise you ran that mile every day until you made your time.

"Practices were two-and-a-half-hour sessions in 90-plus degree weather and we hit all the time. We had the leanest team in the league. Coach Halas believed that a player performed his best at a lighter weight. Our heaviest lineman was Doug at 280, and Halas wanted him at 260. At that he was really sculpted.

"We had to be exactly what they wanted us to be. Some of our linemen would be coming in for weigh-ins with bags of food in their hands so they could eat right after they were done. Halas had me down at 220 pounds. I came in and for some reason I got on the scale and only weighed 218 and thought, oh my. I drank some water, got back on the scale but it barely budged.

"I scrounged through the locker room and I found a wrench. I stuck it inside my shorts and taped it on my stomach and came back in. Halas says, 'OK, get on the scale.' Well, now I'm 221. He says, 'That'll cost you $25 for being a pound over.'"

CHAPTER 8

THE ORIGINAL MONSTERS

The Bears dominated much of professional football from its earliest days. But that dominance reached legendary levels in the 1940s with the arrival of Sid Luckman, Bulldog Turner, George McAfee and others who took the foundation that George Halas had built and put something atop it that still is the stuff of legend.

73-0

This game defined the Bears for decades and was perhaps the embodiment of all that came to be known as "The Monsters of the Midway." On Dec. 8, 1940 the Bears of George Halas played a game for the football ages, destroying the Washington Redskins of George Marshall 73-0.

Ten different Bears scored touchdowns, and by the end of the game, the officials asked the Bears to stop kicking the extra points because, with the kicks sailing up into the stands and staying there, they were about out of footballs. The defense intercepted eight passes and ran three back for touchdowns. The Bears rushed for 372 yards to three for the 'Skins.

When the final gun sounded, someone remarked, "Marshall just shot himself."

The stage had been set, however, three weeks earlier.

"We were in Washington and they'd beat us [7-3] but we had a play there in the latter part of the game where we thought they held Bill Osmanski on a pass that would have been the winning touchdown," said Hall of Fame halfback George McAfee. "We were frustrated about not getting the call, and Mr. Marshall said after the game that we were crybabies." Bad idea.

"When we left Washington, we were one mad bunch of Bears."

Halas, being a master psychologist, fueled the rage by putting the press clippings on the clubhouse wall the Monday before the championship game.

"That was really the big buildup for that game," halfback Ray Nolting said, laughing. "I don't think a more determined bunch of football players ever existed."

They took it out on the Redskins. In a big, big hurry.

On the first play of the game, from the Bears' 24, quarterback Sid Luckman sent Nolting in motion and gave the ball to McAfee, who picked up eight yards between guard and tackle. But Luckman had seen what he wanted: the Washington linebacker followed Nolting.

Luckman sent McAfee in motion on the second play, took Turner's snap and reverse-pivoted, handing the ball to Osmanski. "Bill was really driving when I handed that ball to him," Luckman recalled afterwards. "I knew he was going someplace in a big hurry."

Osmanski started off tackle, dipped inside, then swung wide behind George Musso, pulling from his right guard spot, and was off. Near the Washington 35, Redskins Jimmy Johnson and Ed "Chug" Justice closed in for the tackle, but Bears right end George Wilson hurled himself into both would-be tacklers, obliterating them in one of the most famous blocks in NFL history.

Osmanski went the rest of the way to complete the 68-yard TD run.

Newspaper columnist and 1960s Bears announcer Irv Kupcinet was a referee in that game. "Irv said he made a key block on one of the Redskins for us too," McAfee said, laughing.

The Redskins weren't laughing. Washington quarterback Slingin' Sammy Baugh found end Charlie Malone all alone deep in the Chicago secondary and laid the ball right in Malone's hands. But Malone dropped the sure score and the Redskins were headed for a shutout.

Asked later if Malone making that catch would have changed the outcome of the game, Baugh reflected. "Sure," he replied. "The score would have been 73-7."

At one point Halas considered not running up the score. But he'd reminded his boys at halftime that

Marshall also had called them "strictly a first-half ball club." Another bad idea by Marshall.

"When we got around 40 points, George [Halas] tried to pull off the dogs and not run the score up," Nolting said. "But when it got near 60 he was all for it again and said just go ahead. And we did."

"It was such a big surprise the way it went, we didn't quite realize everything that was going on until the next day or two, even a couple years later," remembered Clyde "Bulldog" Turner, the big center and linebacker who would go into the Hall of Fame along with five other teammates from that game. "Not only were we looking good that day, they were looking bad, too."

Luckman remembered that "George Preston Marshall, owner of the Redskins, came out with these blaring headlines, 'The Bears are front runners, the Bears are crybabies, that Washington was going to destroy them.'

"He said, 'Here it is; this is what the Redskins think of you. My opinion of you is that you're the greatest football team in America. But you've got to prove it to yourself and you've got to prove it to your families and to the fans of America.'

"And we devastated them."

Wartime

Many Bears, including George Halas, spent time in the service during World War II. Don't tell them that "football is like war." No Packer on his meanest day compared to a German or Japanese soldier with a rifle.

Defensive lineman Jack Karwales, who played for the Bears and then for the world champion Chicago Cardinals in 1947, was stationed in the Pacific, on the island of Tinian, when the first atomic bomb arrived, as did the B-29 bomber Enola Gay under Paul Tibbets.

"The bomb came over by ship and we unloaded it at the dock," Karwales said. "All of a sudden we had all these guys in khaki with no insignia, no medals, no rank. We wondered what the hell they were doing there.

"Leo Balarini was the head chef on the island and he was from Chicago. He came over to my tent and says, 'Jack, c'mon over. We're feeding the guys who are flying the Enola Gay, Tibbets and his guys.' So I went over to be there just to be part of it.

"It was an early flight to get out of there and boy, were they loaded down. They were overweight with ammunition and the bomb and I saw them take off and come back. We were all tuned into Tokyo Rose and we knew about when they'd probably drop the bomb. All of a sudden she went berserk and the radio went out of whack and we knew that was it.

"We knew we were part of something big, but nobody knew it was going to be that big."

Orientation

Hall of Fame tackle and linebacker George Connor was a rookie in 1948 and was on the sideline for his first game. Starting tackle Fred Davis told Connor to watch him and whenever Davis put up his hand, Connor was to get his helmet and come in on the next play and give Davis a break.

Davis finally raised his right hand and in went Connor. The defensive lineman opposite him proceeded to punch him square in the mouth on the first play. Connor dismissed the gesture as a consequence of not wearing a facemask and as an effort at intimidation.

In the second half, Davis again raised his hand, Connor went in and a different defender smacked him in the mouth. Connor thought afterwards that it might be some anti-Notre Dame bias. He found out otherwise the next Sunday.

Instead of going for his helmet when Davis signaled, Connor watched the next play. What he saw was Davis reach out and punch his opposite number in the mouth as soon as the ball was snapped, then trot off the field, leaving Connor to deal with the incensed opponent.

Health Risk

Defensive lineman Jack Karwales had to overcome an unusual surgical problem in order to get on the field against NFL players.

Karwales, then in the military, was circumsised in 1943. "They'd line you up and if you needed it, they'd chop ya'," Karwales said. "So I'm lying in bed and I get this offer to go to the All-Star Game and I'm real weak. And then the base commander wouldn't let me go.

When I got out of the hospital, I went into his office and closed the door so hard I knocked all the glass out of the door. He froze and I said, 'You son of a bitch!' And he was a major and I was a PFC. I was so hot."

A Carmelite priest from Chicago who was assigned to Key Field in Meridian, Miss., where Karwales was stationed, got Karwales out of that predicament and he came up to Chicago. But when Karwales got to Northwestern he came a day late and wasn't in the best of shape after his "procedure."

"I am weaker than hell but I check in and get my uniform, my sweatsuits and all that, and go on out to practice," Karwales said. "Harry Stuhldreher, who's coaching at Wisconsin, has everybody in session, talking to the whole group and I barely made it out onto the field. He yells, 'Kavallas'—he had this funny way of talking—'start running around the field and don't stop 'til I tell you to.'

"I start circling and circling and they're doing a scrimmage and he calls me into the group. I had shin splints so bad I couldn't walk up the stairs after practice at Dyche Stadium, where we were sleeping. 'What's the matter, Kavallas, don'tcha want to play?' Stuhldreher demanded."

"Coach," Karwales said, "don't give me that shit. Why am I here? I just got circumcised and I was in the hospital."

"Why didn't you tell me?" Stuhldreher asked.

"I didn't think that would matter," Karwales said simply.

So they "shot me with a preparation of snake oil or venom or some damn thing in both of my shins," Karwales said, "and that relieved the pressure."

Momma Luckman

On Nov. 14, 1943, in what would be another NFL championship season for the Monsters of the Midway, Sid Luckman threw a record-tying seven touchdown passes in the Bears' 56-7 victory. But his mother wasn't impressed.

"That's one of the few games my mother ever went to," Luckman said. "She was always afraid I would play and get hurt. I was running with the ball and she was sitting with my brother and sister, and yelling, 'Please, Sid, please, Sid, give them the ball. Let them run with the ball.'"

Stat Man

The NFL didn't start keeping track of sacks as a statistic until 1982, although the term was coined by Hall of Fame defensive end David "Deacon" Jones in the 1960s. The sack totals of bygone eras are fun to imagine, although there would have been fewer sacks if for no other reason than the offenses of the pre-1960 NFL were run-based.

Still...

"As a defensive end, they didn't keep track of sacks as a statistic," said Ed Sprinkle, a Bears defensive end from 1944-55. "They didn't have them. They were just another tackle. Bulldog [Turner] and I always knew that the opportunity was not always there for you to make a lot of tackles, too. If you were right defensive end and they ran to their right all the time, you might not get the opportunity to make a tackle.

"But in one game against Baltimore I made five sacks. Back then, though, they were just counted as tackles. There were a lot of things written about me over the years, but I do know that if they had kept track of sacks then the way they do now, I'd have been right up at the head of the class.

"But I looked at it as just going out there to play a game and try to win. I get a kick out of guys now, when the quarterback falls down and they run over and tap him on the ground, then turn around and point to themselves, like 'That's *my* sack.'"

Bronk

Bronco Nagurski was the standard of rugged for the era in which the Bears formed their "Monsters of the Midway" persona. At 230 pounds, he could deliver a blow like few others in his time.

He could take one like few others too.

In 1930, his rookie season, Nagurski was being hit hard in a rough game at Wrigley Field, a venue notable for its being a little short for a football field. The line defining the back of one end zone in fact went up onto the bricks of the outfield wall in one corner.

With the Bears in possession at the opposing two-yard line, Nagurski took the handoff and blasted head-down into the line. He smashed through one tackler, then a second, then hit the goal post, in those days sitting at the goal line. Bronk didn't stop, just kept churning off the post and powered through the end zone and into the brick wall, which finally brought him to a dazed stop.

Coming over to the Bears bench on the sideline he was asked if he was OK.

"Yeah, I am," he said, shaking his head, "but that last guy really hit me."

Tough Guy

Hall of Fame center Clyde "Bulldog" Turner is supposed to have fallen out of a third-story window of a hotel and was saved when he hit an awning that broke his fall. A policeman came running up as Turner was collecting himself and asked, "What happened here?"

"I don't know," Turner answered. "I just got here myself."

Teammate Ed Sprinkle remembers Turner. "There was a lot of camaraderie back then with your teammates," Sprinkle says. "It was just fun to be a Bear and play in the NFL. Bulldog Turner was one of my better friends; we went to the same school, Hardin-

Bronco Nagurski *AP/WWP*

Simmons, and we roomed together on the road for eight years. He was a kind of guy who loved to drink and I tried to take care of him a lot. We'd get into some funny situations.

"He was one of those guys who wakes up all beat up and bandaged up and says, 'How'd I get here?' You tell him, 'You bet people you could go out the window and walk around the building.' He'd say, 'Why didn't you stop me?' I'd tell him, 'Stop ya? I bet you could do it!'"

Salesman

Playing for George Halas probably meant needing a second source of income besides football, as it did for a lot of pro football players before the money of television. Players got a couple of tickets to give away, but tackle Lee Artoe had other ideas.

Artoe wouldn't give his tickets away; he'd go out in front of the stadium and sell the tickets. Then he'd come in late and Halas would chew him out. "You out there again selling the damn tickets?"

Boys, Boys

Being teammates was no assurance of being accorded anything close to civil courtesy. Sometimes just the opposite.

"My first scrimmage, you're a newcomer and getting established, and I'm playing against Ed Sprinkle," said Jack Karwales. "We were having a charity game to raise money for the school system in Renssalaer. And he gives me a shot in the head. We lined up and as I go by him he gives me an elbow right in the side of the head.

"I grabbed him, we went down and I stepped all over him with my cleats. Walked right on. I missed his face but I got him in the chest. Sprinkle would clothesline guys, hit them in the neck and he'd do it to his own guys in practice. He was a dirty son of a bitch.

"Sprinkle and I were running a golf tournament together and he got some people to donate equipment. And then he kept it all! Everything. His garage was packed full of the stuff. So I go to Ed and says, 'Ed, when are we going to give this out and give it to the players?' He says, 'I'll take care of it, Jack.' The son of a bitch never did."

The Claw

Sprinkle's clothesline had a name: The Claw. "I'd come in on the quarterback and have a blocker on me. And there'd come the halfback going out for a pass. So I'd jump or reach out and hook 'em.

"When you got into the pros, the coaches don't have time to teach you how to play football. So nobody ever told me how to play defensive end, do this or that. They would tell you in the defenses where to play or what to do, but how you played was more or less something you developed on your own.

"I played in a 'down' stance, a three-point stance, but a lot of defensive ends then didn't. I'd always key off the guard. If the guard pulled out and was coming down the line to hit me, I could see him and would go in and hit him instead. If the ball carrier went wide, then I used the momentum off him to take myself wide and keep the ball carrier from going wide. But stuff like that I more or less learned myself."

Sprinkle doesn't like to be reminded of his reputation as one of the league's dirtiest players. He also vehemently disagrees with that assessment of him as a player.

"I get very agitated about that because I don't think I was a dirty football player," Sprinkle says. "I didn't deserve that. Somebody who never saw you play will say, 'Oh, you were a dirty player.' It rankles you a little bit. I played hard and I played mean and what the hell, if they call that dirty, then so be it. That's not how I thought about it.

"If I was rushing a quarterback and had a chance to hit him, if he's running, I'd hit him. That's part of the job."

Much is made of the toughness and crustiness of past-era players toward each other, and many don't like the shows of friendship among players on the field before and after games. But truth be told, it wasn't all animosity among combatants back then, even among the toughest.

"Lou Creekmur [Hall of Fame guard for the Detroit Lions] would be blocking on me and he weighed 260-270. He'd be coming at me, and I weighed 210 and had to beat the guy some way. Well, we'd always meet down at The Cottage on Sunday night and Lou was in there laughing, and said, 'Well, you got me on that one today.' I asked him what he meant and he said, 'You knocked my tooth out.'

"But it wasn't animosity or anything like that. We left it all on the field. He once said he came out blocking me, raised his head up and all he could see was two feet coming right in his face. That was a really outstanding Lions line. Dick Stanfel was the other guard and he was the MVP of a championship game. Dick was an All-Pro player and I think he was even better than Lou. Lou was good, but Stanfel was outstanding.

"I had guards coming out at 250 with a couple of steps first and I knocked guards on their backs. It was just the way I played. Abe Gibron was a heck of a blocker and Marion Motley was maybe 250 and blocking on me, so I had to really work to get around them to get to Otto Graham. One time Abe came out at me and I just hurdled him, over top of him. Graham was rolling out my way and I was able to get a sack of Graham, but there weren't too many against him because he had a pretty good line.

"Abe and Lou Groza were the left side of their line and Lou was blocking on me. But then he told Abe to switch after a while, that he didn't want to block on me. So he switched and had Abe pull and block me.

"We'd play Philadelphia and Steve Van Buren, who had some great days and great games. But most of the time he wasn't running my way. He'd run the other way. But he was big and he was a tough one to tackle.

"The Cardinals had that so-called 'Dream Backfield,' with Paul Christman, and he didn't like getting hit. One time supposedly he said he fired the ball in my face and knocked me out. It never happened. If it had, I would have tried to kill him."

What Might Have Been?

World War II took many of the great Bears and members of other NFL teams into the horrors of battle and far, far from football. Sid Luckman was on a tanker in the North Atlantic where he dodged German U-boats and mines. George McAfee went into the navy in 1942, as did Halas. Bill Osmanski, who'd scored the first touchdown in the 73-0 game, served as a navy dentist with the Marines on Okinawa.

"I remember asking Mr. Halas once, that had the war not come along, just how good could that [1940s] team have been?" McAfee mused. "He thought about it a minute and said, 'There's no telling.' And I believe he was right."

Sprinkle's Day

Ed Sprinkle was one of the most feared players in the game during his 1944-55 career. He was out of tiny Hardin-Simmons in Texas, the same school that produced Clyde "Bulldog" Turner, and played the game never asking nor giving any quarter.

He would go to the Pro Bowl (then just the NFL All-Star Game) the first three years of its existence (1951-53) and again in 1955. But his breakthrough came in the best of all possible venues, the NFL championship game of 1946, won by the Bears 24-14. Sprinkle provided the game's violent turning point.

"We played against the Giants in the championship game in 1946 and that was one of the best-remembered games I ever played in," Sprinkle says. "They had switched me to right defensive end in that game. We'd had an All-Pro defensive end, George Wilson, who played right end, and they wanted to put me at left end. I said, no, I played right end. I'd played some defensive end in college and at the Naval Academy, so they moved him to left end and put me at right end."

Unfortunately for the Giants. They were without fullback Merle Hapes, who was suspended for failing to report a bribe attempt, and Giants quarterback Frank Filchock could have used Hapes' pass protection. In the first quarter, Filchock dropped to pass and Sprinkle came in right over a blocker and hit him with a blow that broke his nose. It also caused the ball to sputter out of his hands and up in the air where it was grabbed by defensive back Dante Margnani, who returned it 19 yards to give the Bears a 14-0 lead.

"Dante almost walked in for the touchdown," Sprinkle said. "I had a really good game and that was the game that really set my career off."

CHAPTER 9

THE OLD MAN

George Halas isn't part of NFL history; he is NFL history. He was there to start the whole thing; he nurtured it, defined it and helped create an American institution. And why not? He's one himself.

Halas may have helped found the National Football League, but that didn't always get him special consideration once the games started. Halas was ranting and raging on the sideline during one 1920s contest when referee Jim Durfee suddenly marched off a five-yard penalty.

"What the hell's that for?" Halas bellowed.

"Coaching from the sidelines," Durfee hollered back, citing what was then against the rules.

"Well, that's how stupid you are," Halas roared. "It's a 15-yard penalty, not five!"

"George," Durfee said, ending the discussion, "your coaching's only worth five."

Tough Guy–Tough Coach

Hall of Famer George Connor was kicked in the head by a Packer and needed stitches in his chin at halftime. He went into the boiler room of Lambeau Field, then called City Stadium, to have the cut stitched up.

When he was finished, he was a little late for the second half and the stadium gates were padlocked. Connor yelled to some Bears fans in the stadium, who came down and got into a fight with stadium people to get the gate open.

Connor ran into the stadium, but the Bears were on the other side of the field, play was going on, and he had to wait for a timeout to run across to their side.

"Where have you been?" Halas yelled. "You're late. That'll cost you $50."

Cash Crunch and a Mother's Love

Halas would come to be the cornerstone on which the National Football League was built. But very early in its history, the Bears were within minutes of being taken from Halas.

It almost happened in 1933. Profits were thin in the early years. Halas sold cars to make a living; co-owner Dutch Sternaman pumped gas. In 1932

Sternaman needed money to pay the mortgages on an apartment house and gas station, so he offered to sell Halas his share of the Bears for $38,000. Halas went for it.

Halas agreed to make his final payment in 1933, with the deal being that if he could not come up with the full amount, everything would revert to Sternaman. Halas would be out. The Bears in fact won the NFL championship in 1932 too.

But they lost money, a deficit of $18,000. So when the final payment on the buyout of the Bears was due, Halas was short.

Fortunately, Halas had a friend in Charlie Bidwill, who would eventually buy the rival Chicago Cardinals. Bidwill put up $5,000 to buy Bears stock from Halas. Bidwill also helped set up a bank loan from a bank that was closed because of the Depression.

Halas got $5,000 from his mother, Barbara, a widow who lived on the income from a grocery store she'd opened after Halas' father suffered a stroke. Her Bohemian duck was Halas' favorite dish growing up, and now she was serving him something even more important.

Halas faced a noon deadline. If the final money wasn't in the office of Sternaman's attorney by noon on Aug. 9, 1933, the Bears would belong to Sternaman, who would put the franchise up for sale. By 11 a.m. that day, Halas was still $5,000 short.

Then C. K. Anderson, president of First National Bank in Antioch, phoned Halas to say he'd learned Halas desperately needed funds. He agreed to lend Halas the money and Halas ran over to the bank's office in Chicago to get the check. Halas picked up the money and ran to the office of Sternaman's lawyer, getting the money to him at 10 minutes before noon, just before the fire sale would have started.

Halas had his Bears.

Negotiating with Halas

Winning the '63 world championship didn't loosen Halas' legendarily tight purse strings. Mike Ditka once remarked that the Old Man threw nickels around like they were manhole covers, and few of his players would disagree.

The Bears had just won the world championship, and the players were waiting to see what they'd get as a bonus, knowing that Packers players got things from Lombardi and other teams gave things to the players. Bears players instead got a paperweight, not from Halas and the Bears, but from Mayor Richard Daley. "That's all we got, from the mayor, not the team," fumed Ed O'Bradovich.

"Everybody wanted out or more money," O'Bradovich said. "So I waited to find the time to make my move. It was about 9 or 10 o' clock at night and Halas said, 'Sure kid, c'mon in.' I was making about $11,000 a year. I said I wanted a $5,000 raise."

"No," Halas said.

"What do you mean by 'no'?" O'Bradovich asked.

"Just what I told you—no."

O'Bradovich reminded Halas that they'd won the world championship and that in the title game against the New York Giants he'd intercepted the Y.A. Tittle pass to set up the winning touchdown.

"Anybody could've done that," Halas barked.

"Nobody did it but me and that pass led to the winning touchdown," O'Bradovich countered. "I want my $5,000 raise, bonus or whatever you want to call it, or get rid of me."

"No, you're not getting the $5,000, and we're not getting rid of you," Halas declared.

O'Bradovich continued to make his case until Halas ordered him out of the room. As he got to the door, Halas got in the last word, as always.

"Normally when a player leaves camp, it's $100 a day," Halas said. "But for you, I'll make it $200. Have a nice night, kid."

O'Bradovich was a veteran in more ways than one. "I think in my years I held out four times," he said, "and lost every time."

The Book

Halas taught O'Bradovich the NFL meaning of "creative bookkeeping." Going into one negotiation, O'Bradovich had what he thought was one of his better years. But what Halas did was keep The Book, the grading book he'd pull out when it came time to discuss how someone had played, and to "show" the player how bad he'd really been.

O'Bradovich went to see him again about a raise, because he was getting interest from the Dallas Cowboys. He wanted $10,000 from Halas. He walked in and said, "Before we start the conversation, pull the book out."

"All right, kid," Halas said, pulling out the book.

O'Bradovich had been through this before with the Old Man, with Halas going game by game in his ledger and "documenting" missed tackles and other sundry misdeeds, concluding, "according to this, you're one of the worst defensive linemen we've got. I can't give you the raise."

"He'd do that to everybody," O'Bradovich says. "No one knew where the grades came from and everyone suspected the Old Man had more than one set of so-called books."

O'Bradovich told Halas to go right to No. 87 and he pointed out to Halas game by game what he'd done. "According to this," O'Bradovich concluded, "I was the best defensive lineman you had."

Halas looked up from the book at O'Bradovich. "You know what you can do with these grades?" Halas announced. "You can take 'em and stick 'em up your ass. Thank you very much and don't let the door hit you in the ass."

Halas and "Big Man"

Halas met his equal in defensive end Doug Atkins. The two went at each other constantly, with Atkins knowing how to get under Halas' skin and being good enough on the field that Halas wasn't going to put his foot down too hard. Besides, he couldn't always be sure exactly what Big Man would do anyway.

Playing the Minnesota Vikings, Atkins had been out the night before and had a few too many and wasn't feeling too well. The Vikings were doing a number on the Bears and Atkins was throwing up in the huddle, sick as a dog.

At halftime the players had orange slices and Cokes. Halas always had two Coke bottles prepared for him for halftime, special Cokes with Early Times whiskey mixed in. Atkins was heaving in the huddle and still killing Vikings left tackle Grady Alderman, throwing him through the air like a clown jumping off a board.

At halftime, Atkins came in and grabbed one of Halas' bottles of Coke and liquor. He downed it without missing a beat as the trainer started yelling. Then Halas walked in and saw the one bottle left, and it was in Atkins' massive paw.

So, with the Bears getting pummeled on the scoreboard, the main thing at that halftime was not some adjustment, but rather that little bottle. Perhaps the greatest defensive end in NFL history and the founder of the league (and one of its genuine legends) started arguing. Halas grabbed Atkins' hand with the bottle in it and started tugging. Atkins tugged back, and the two tugged away until finally Atkins muttered, "Oh, take it, ya' old fuck."

On the Run

Halas in his autobiography *Halas on Halas* put some of the finances and emotions of the early game in perspective in his team's first-ever season. Fans became emotional about their local team then not so much out of allegiance (the league hadn't been around that long, and there was no TV or radio in the beginning) as out of betting results.

His Staleys had beaten the Rock Island Independents 7-0 in a game that had been attended by a legion of Staley fans who'd chartered a train, and those fans had cleaned up in an upset over a strong team. When the Bears returned for another game three weeks later, Halas figured feelings were running high, so he lodged the team at the Hotel Davenport, across the river from Rock Island.

Word from a number of gamblers was that Bears tough guy George Trafton, whose career at Notre Dame ended when Knute Rockne caught him playing semipro ball, would be knocked out of the game as early as the first quarter. It didn't quite work that way.

Trafton proceeded to knock four Rockford players out of the game in the first 12 plays, the last being Independents fullback Fred Chicken, initially deemed the one most likely to do in Trafton. The Rock Island doctor returned Chicken to consciousness but with 19 stitches in Chicken's scalp and a cast on his broken wrist.

This scarcely improved the mood of the Rock Island fans. So as the 0-0 game wound down to its last play, Halas devised a play with Trafton carrying the ball through an exit to get him out of the stadium. The gun went off (presumably not one fired by a Rock Island fan,) and Trafton was through the exit, quickly donning a sweatshirt that was provided underneath the stands to disguise his number. Trafton jumped into a car and got across the bridge and the state line to Iowa.

The Bears' share of the gate receipts from that game has been pegged at different amounts, sometimes $3,000, other times $7,000. Whatever the amount, it was in cash, so at the Hotel Davenport, Halas gave the money to Trafton to bring to the team's train. His reasoning: "I knew if we did encounter obstreperous Rock Island fans, I would run for the money but Trafton would run for his life."

Good Idea

Halas was an innovator of epic proportions and also of little creations if they offered an advantage. He got an idea that it would be possible to install tiny radio receivers in players' helmets and met with Motorola founder Bob Galvin and others, coming up with a concept far ahead of its time.

Halas had a wire buried around the football field to act as a transmitter and put receivers in the helmets of the quarterback and the defensive captain. For three games he was able to radio in instructions. Then the league got wind of his breakthrough and banned its operation.

Today every NFL quarterback has a receiver in his helmet that allows him to get his plays and instructions from coaches on the bench.

Money Matters

Ed O'Bradovich thought he'd had a pretty good season one year and decided he needed a $4,000 raise from Halas to sign his next contract. They sat down, O'Bradovich made his pitch, and Halas answered that, well, O'Bradovich really hadn't played all that well, and besides, the Bears were losing money. O'Bradovich, ever the team player, dropped his demand to $3,000.

Halas declared, though, that O'Bradovich had been skirt-chasing, running with riff-raff, and not doing his workouts and calisthenics the way he was supposed to. OK, O'Bradovich figured, make it $2,000.

The haggling went on and O'Bradovich said $1,000 would do it. Halas hemmed and hawed and poor-mouthed until O'Bradovich stood up and threw in the towel.

"Hey, Coach," O'Bradovich concluded, "let me give you a check for $500."

Sneaking Up

Halas would tell the story on himself during his playing days of a painful encounter with Joe Guyon, a full-blooded Native American then playing for the New York Giants. Guyon in 1927 was quarterbacking the Giants and faded back to pass as Halas bore in from his spot at right defensive end.

Halas had visions of a blind-side hit (the term "sack" wasn't invented yet; that would be coined by Los Angeles Rams Hall of Fame end David "Deacon" Jones in the 1960s) and maybe a fumble.

Guyon got off the pass at the last second, then spun to greet Halas with a knee that broke several of Halas' ribs. Guyon, who'd played with the Carlisle Indians and other teams with the great Jim Thorpe, took a look at the writhing Halas on the ground and shook his head.

"C'mon, Halas," Guyon admonished. "You should know better than to try to sneak up on an Indian."

Chapter 10

WALTER

Walter Payton set records and defined the Bears for more than a decade. He was the symbol of a team and eventually of a city. He was beyond description, except perhaps for the simplest:

"He was the greatest Bear of all."—Mike Ditka

Walter Payton played for the Bears from 1975, when he was the fourth pick of the first round out of Jackson State, until 1987.When he died in 1999, more than just the football world cried.

The Bears and the city of Chicago held a moving tribute to Walter on the Saturday following his death. Former teammates, team officials and current players all said what was on their minds and hearts, and the crowd of more than 20,000 in Soldier Field shared some of the sadness of the moment as well as the magic of Walter.

The most poignant moment came not from a coach or member of the Bears' offense. Defensive end Dan

Hampton, himself voted to Pro Football's Hall of Fame in 2002, was one of the toughest of a tough bunch of players, but the memory of Walter was more than he could bear up to as his comments came to a close.

His voice choked with emotion, Hampton looked both back and ahead as he recalled teammate Walter Payton.

"I remember this guy playing on this field and leaving it on this field time after time," Hampton said, struggling for control as his hands shook and his voice broke slightly as he spoke to the crowd at Soldier Field.

He paused as tears came to his eyes. Then he finished: "I have a little girl [who's] four years old. Ten years from now, when she asks me about the Chicago Bears, I'll tell her about a championship and I'll tell her about great teams, great teammates and great coaches, and how great it was to be a part of it.

"But the first thing I'll tell her about is Walter Payton."

* * * *

Walter took fun seriously. Once, after sprinkling powdered sugar in his moustache, Walter burst into a meeting on drugs being conducted by an NFL official. "Ain't no cocaine on this team!" Walter yelled.

* * * *

Defensive end Clyde Simmons, who finished his career as a Bear in 2000, had the rare distinction among his Chicago teammates of being the only one who played on the same field with Walter. Simmons was a rookie with the Philadelphia Eagles in 1986, and his second NFL game was against the Bears, when the Eagles came to Soldier Field. The game was a hard-fought, 13-10 contest that was settled in overtime by a Kevin Butler field goal.

Simmons, a backup at the time who ultimately would go on to become one of the NFL's all-time great pass rushers, got in the Bears game briefly and made his first career tackle: a stop of the Bears' Hall of Fame running back.

Later the tackle came up in conversation, "and the first thing that came to Payton's mind was, 'Did you hit me hard?'" Simmons said. "I said, 'No, I was just happy to hold on.'"

"You have to understand how special it is to be a Chicago Bear, and Walter Payton always did," Hampton said, recalling Payton's simple order to teammates every week: "'Play your [butt] off.' That's all he ever wanted from us."

* * * *

Safety Dave Duerson was voted to his first Pro Bowl in Hawaii after the Bears' Super Bowl victory. He went out for his first practice, enjoying the warmth, but was beset by a different kind of warmth, courtesy of Walter.

"Walter had put some unscented liquid heat in my [athletic supporter]," Duerson says, shaking his head. "Let's just say, it was a very hot afternoon in warm, sunny Hawaii."

* * * *

Training camp was prime time for the legendary Payton mischief.

Defensive tackle Jim Osborne recalled the fatigue and exhaustion from two-a-day practices in camp that left tired players in a deep sleep at night. Payton, though, was not above dipping into his endless supply of fireworks and detonating a large firecracker in the dorm, jolting his teammates out of whatever sleep they were enjoying.

Yet Walter "never missed practice, was always the first one there ready to go," Osborne said. "He was the guy you knew you could count on. That's what inspired the rest of the team."

* * * *

Tackle James "Big Cat" Williams did not join the Bears until 1991. One of his only career regrets: that he never got to block for Walter. But that doesn't mean he never shared a Payton moment.

"He's probably one of the greatest men I've ever met," Williams says. "Not because of what he did on the field, but because of how he made you feel off it."

Payton once took Williams with him to a north suburban mall for an interview that was supposed to take perhaps 15 minutes. They were there nearly two hours and at one point were in a jewelry store.

"Walter pulled two people aside and tried to sell them wedding bands," Williams recalls, laughing. "For the rest of [the 1999] season I played for Walter, his family and his ex-teammates. I keep them all in my heart and in my head."

* * * *

Walter inspired even Packers fans. Defensive tackle Jim Flanigan, who was drafted by the Bears in the third round of the 1994 draft and had seven seasons in Chicago, grew up in Wisconsin, in the middle of Packers country.

One day Flanigan, then in high school, learned of Payton's legendary workout regimen that included grueling runs up a steep hill in Barrington. Flanigan's father played for the Packers, and Flanigan would play for Green Bay himself after the Bears released him in 2000. There was a ski hill near Flanigan's boyhood home and he went there to run to try to emulate Payton.

* * * *

Walter, who was a mixture of power and grace matched only by Jim Brown, once explained one of his training techniques to Don Pierson of the *Chicago Tribune*.

Walter did extensive running in sand as part of his training, explaining that "if you have to come under control to make a cut, the pursuit will catch you. In the sand, you have to move one leg before the other is planted. It makes all your muscles work. Sometimes when I'm done even my neck will be aching."

Because of the ways he trained, Walter sometimes had everyone else's neck aching.

* * * *

Walter was a race car driver, amateur and professional. He owned a restaurant and was an entrepreneur. He invested in forest land and nursing homes. He leased heavy equipment and made up to $1 million a year giving motivational speeches. But there was more to Walter.

"People see what they want to see," Walter said. "They look at me and say, 'He's a black man. He's a football player. He's a running back. He's a Chicago Bear.' But I'm more than all that. I'm a father. I'm a husband. I'm a citizen. I'm a person who is willing to give his all. That's how I want to be remembered."

* * * *

How great were Walter's accomplishments? Twelve years after Walter retired, he still held or shared eight NFL records, including the all-time rushing record of 16,726 yards. (This record was finally broken by Dallas' Emmitt Smith in 2002.)

* * * *

Mike Ditka inherited Walter when he came to coach the Bears in 1982. He knew what he had, and at Walter's memorial service said it as well as anyone in attendance. Ditka called Walter "the best runner, blocker, teammate and friend I've ever seen. Truly the best football player I've ever seen. Coach [George] Halas is saying, 'Hey, I've finally got the greatest Bear of all.'"

* * * *

NFL television analyst John Madden offered to end all arguments about who was the greatest. "Walter Payton was the greatest," he said. "If you wanted yards, you'd want Walter Payton. Who do you want to block? Walter Payton. If you wanted someone to catch, Walter Payton. He played on some bad teams. How about if you want somebody to make a tackle after an interception? One year he had 18."

* * * *

Walter's older brother Eddie, himself a kick returner for four NFL teams, recalled a Mississippi gas station attendant mistaking him for Walter and giving him a free tank. In a high-pitched voice imitating Walter, Eddie told the man, "If you're ever in Chicago, look me up."

* * * *

Despite the increased emphasis on passing, football's rushing record has always been something extra special, like the home-run record of first Babe Ruth, then Henry Aaron, or the consecutive-game streak of Lou Gehrig and now Cal Ripken. When Walter broke Jim Brown's record, he got a call from President Ronald Reagan in the locker room afterwards.

"The check's in the mail," Payton joked.

* * * *

Walter took whatever edge he could and he'd do whatever he could to stretch things a little, but usually with a warrior's sense of humor. Most of his runs ended with his hand darting out of the pile and placing the ball a foot or two farther down the field. He was said to have kidded that he'd added 100 yards to his career total with those sneaky inches.

Most of the time he'd be caught and the ball placed where it belonged. Once he joked to a vigilant official who was spotting the ball, "How do you expect me to catch Jim Brown if you do that?"

* * * *

Walter and his financial advisors managed his money and investments very well, but not all financial matters were easy. After Walter gained 1,395 yards in the first 16-game season, he sought $513,000

in salary from the Bears, which was 70 percent of O. J. Simpson's pay envelope of $733,000, tops in the NFL. The Bears offered $391,000 a year. Eventually Walter agreed to a three-year deal averaging $425,000 a year

Walter Payton picks his spot against the Lions. ***AP/WWP***

plus some incentives, but he understandably wasn't particularly pleased.

"The thing is, people want me to beat all O. J.'s records," Walter said. "'Beat this, beat that.' Why don't they want me to beat his salary? Tell me that. It's like telling a little kid in baseball, 'I want you to catch every ball and when this guy comes up, let him go.' I can't do that."

* * * *

Walter set the NFL single-game rushing record with 275 yards against the Minnesota Vikings on Nov. 20, 1977, a record since broken by Corey Dillon of the Cincinnati Bengals. Of Hall of Fame tight end John Mackey it was often said, "the lucky ones fell off," and there were those who felt the same about trying to tackle Walter, certainly that day.

"It's similar to trying to rope a calf," said Vikings cornerback Bobby Bryant. "It's hard enough to get your hands on him, and once you do, you wonder if you should have."

* * * *

Gale Sayers was without question one of the NFL's most dangerous and electrifying kick returners off his era and all time, with a peak of 37.7 yards per kickoff return in 1967 (which was second in NFL history but remarkably, didn't lead the league that season; Green Bay Packer (of course) Travis Williams ran 18 kicks back an average of 41.1 yards that same year).

But Walter was a force in his own right with what little time he was given. Walter led the NFL by returning

14 kicks an average of 31.7 yards in 1975, but coach Jack Pardee took him off that duty after he got knocked out against the Rams.

* * * *

In his NFL career Walter missed exactly one game because of an injury. Or did he?

In Walter's rookie season, facing the Pittsburgh Steelers, Jack Pardee and running backs coach Fred O'Connor chose to play former Northwestern star Mike Adamle and gave Walter the day off to rest a sore ankle. That was not how Walter saw it.

"Excuse me; an ankle?" Walter later said. "I played once after getting my ankle taped three times. Taped the skin without prewrap because they said it would hold better. Put on my sock and taped it again. Then I put on my shoe and had it spatted. Gained 100-something yards, scored a couple of touchdowns.

"If you're ready to play and the coach won't let you, is that a missed game?"

* * * *

When Payton broke the all-time rushing mark of Jim Brown, not surprisingly his thoughts at the press conference afterwards were not about himself or Brown:

"The motivating drive for me has been for the athletes who tried but still failed to reach that certain achievement, and also the athlete that didn't get an opportunity to, like the [James] Overstreets, the [Joe] Delaneys and Brian Piccolos. They simplified what the game is made of and what I did out there is a reflection of those guys, because they made the sacrifices as well, and it's a tribute to be able to bestow that honor for them."

Chapter 11

BUTKUS

By acclamation in and out of the NFL, Butkus was the greatest linebacker ever to play pro football. He was a Chicago native who lived and played by a code of violence that few could match, not so much for his much-chronicled malevolence, but for his sheer excellence and force of will. If you played against him, or even with him for that matter, you never forgot it.

The Greatest of All Time

Dick Butkus, who roomed with Ed O'Bradovich, was a dead-serious kid. "He wouldn't know if the sun was out or anything, always had his head down, real serious," O'Bradovich remembered. But he made an impression in a hurry.

Dick Butkus ***AP/WWP***

About halfway through Butkus' first training camp as a rookie in 1965, defensive back Richie Pettitbon was among a group of Bears veterans talking about players. Out of nowhere, Pettitbon offered a prediction: "This guy is going to rewrite the record books," Pettitbon forecast. "He's going to be the greatest of all time."

Lost Soul

The Bears of Butkus' reign may not always have won, but Butkus made a lasting, devastating impression on those who faced him.

"He knocked out L. C. Greenwood on a punt and he knocked out Warren Bankston, who was a fullback and a good special teams player," said Pittsburgh Steelers center Ray Mansfield. "I remember Warren coming over and crying, 'I don't know who I am.'"

Carnivore

"Before you tried to block on Dick, you had to overcome the mystique," said Baltimore Colts center Bill Curry. "It was almost like an odor. He exuded a kind of presence. He dominated a game the way no other player has. He intimidated officials. He'd take the ball away from somebody after the play and shake it in the official's face, and the official pointed their way and gave them the ball. It was awesome."

In the lobby of Halas Hall, the Bears have a display of their Hall of Fame players, including a "description" of Butkus. Minnesota Vikings running back Dave Osborne had been annihilated by Butkus on a sweep against the Bears, and Osborne was asked after the game what had happened to his blocker on the play.

"I don't know," Osborne reflected. "Maybe Butkus ate him."

Brain Power

Butkus was incensed at a call made by official Norm Schacter and raged in the face of the veteran striped shirt. He was shaking his finger and yelling until finally Schacter had had enough.

"Butkus," Schacter warned, "if you don't get your finger out of my face, I'm going to bite your head off."

Butkus stomped off but not before getting the last word. "If you do," Butkus snarled, "you'll have more brains in your stomach than you do in your head."

Roster Management

At one point in the dismal 1-13 campaign of 1969, most of the special teams were staffed with starters. Butkus went to coach Abe Gibron and demanded to know why he, Doug Buffone, Ed O'Bradovich and other front-line players were on first-team special teams when there were guys in uniform who never got on the field.

"We can't trust them," Gibron said simply.

"Then what the hell are they doing on the team?" Butkus bellowed and stormed out.

The Toughest

One day at practice Gale Sayers was asked who the toughest guy he ever played against was. Sayers didn't say a word, just pointed out toward the field: at No. 51.

Sayers had faced Butkus in two college games. "Wherever I went, there he was," Sayers marveled. "I went left. There he was. To my right. There was Butkus."

Los Angeles Rams coach Chuck Knox offered this assessment of Butkus. "He was the kind of linebacker that, when he hit our backs, the back would go back to the huddle and be talking out his earhole and want to know who was supposed to block that crazy sucker..."

Intimidator

"He tried to hurt you," said Dallas Cowboy Dan Reeves. "He was so competitive. Not only did he not want you to gain a yard, he didn't want you to gain an inch. As soon as you had that football, you were the enemy."

"Dick was not satisfied with an ordinary tackle," said New Orleans Saints receiver and eventual Bears special teams coach Dan Abramowicz. He had to hit you, pick you up, drive you, grind you into the ground."

"It was horrifying playing against him because he literally could intimidate an entire offensive team, and

I mean good teams," said Atlanta Falcons running back Alex Hawkins.

"We had a rookie center who was playing against him for the first time," said Dallas Cowboys coach Tom Landry. "And Butkus grunted a lot and growled a lot when he was back there. The first time that rookie center came off his eyes were open wide all the way, he couldn't believe what he was hearing from Butkus. Butkus had him intimidated and he hadn't even blocked him."

Simple Mission

"Dick was an animal," said Hall of Fame defensive end Deacon Jones. "I called him a maniac. A stone maniac. He was a well-conditioned animal and every time he hit you, he tried to put you in the cemetery, not the hospital."

Chapter 12

THE PACK

The Bears would not have become the Bears without the Green Bay Packers. Halas would not have been what he was without Lombardi, Ditka without Forrest Gregg (for better or worse). They live in a rarified place that few can understand who haven't been there themselves. But they can be enjoyed by friends and enemies alike.

The Pen

Agent Steve Zucker was fond of the Bears pen that the Bears had given him to mark the signing of Jim McMahon's first big contract with the team. The pen had worked perfectly for many years for Zucker, through quite a few important deals.

But that changed when defensive tackle Steve McMichael, cut by the Bears in April 1994, was about to sign the contract Zucker negotiated with the Green Bay Packers.

Zucker handed McMichael the pen and Ming initialed a few things, then prepared to sign formally.

"All of a sudden, the pen just stopped writing," Zucker recalls. "It had never done that before, ever. I think a Bears pen just couldn't bring itself to see Steve McMichael become a Green Bay Packer."

Hit Lists

The Packers added a mean note to the storied rivalry when a number of their players came out for a 1986 game wearing white towels from their belts, with various Bears players' numbers listed on the towels. The message: This is a hit list.

The Bears had their own answer for that.

"They came out wearing those towels, hit lists, with our players' number on them, for each guy they were going to 'get,'" says linebacker Jim Morrissey. "Ditka says to us, 'Whoever gets one of those towels, I'll give him a hundred bucks. Bring it to me on the sideline and I'll give you a hundred bucks.'

"So we're running on after special teams and Glen Kozlowski comes running over to Ditka waving towels: 'Hey, coach, I got a couple towels for ya.' I think he went into the Packers' huddle and just started ripping towels off everybody."

"The Payton Game"

In 1999, the day after a Soldier Field memorial service for Walter Payton, the Bears appeared headed for yet another loss to the Green Bay Packers. But Walter had other ideas.

Bears kicker Chris Boniol pushed a 32-yard field-goal try wide left with five minutes, 56 seconds remaining. But some things are simply meant to be, and after an emotional week following Payton's death Monday from liver cancer, Bears players believed a victory was somehow waiting for them.

They had no idea that Walter himself may have had a hand in making that dream happen.

"I don't want to say that we came out and dedicated the game to Walter," said receiver Bobby Engram. "But we did feel his presence."

So did the Packers. They trailed the Bears 14-13 when Brett Favre drove the team down inside the Chicago 20 and Ryan Longwell prepared to kick a 28-yard field goal that would give Green Bay a 16-14 victory that would have been the 11th straight in a storied rivalry.

The ball was snapped and placed down. Longwell approached and delivered the kick. It started on its trip toward the uprights in the north end zone. It was up to the heavens at that point.

Defensive lineman Bryan Robinson jumped up and got a hand on the ball, deflecting it far short of the goal line where it was recovered by safety Tony Parrish.

Walter Payton *AP/WWP*

Afterwards, Robinson was not about to claim sole credit for his game-saving play.

"I think Walter Payton actually picked me up," Robinson said, "because I know I can't jump that high."

Robinson wasn't the only Bear stunned by what he saw and experienced that day. "I have just one word," said running back James Allen. "It's sweet. 'Sweetness.'"

Said coach Dick Jauron: "We've got to believe Walter Payton had a hand in the final play."

A Little Respect, Please?

Bears and Packers players didn't always especially care for each other. But it wasn't enough that many Packers and Bears players haven't always been the best of friends. Sometimes that pent-up emotion from both teams erupted into occasional extracurricular activity.

"The lack of respect is what got to me," said tackle Mike Wells. "It just seemed like we had everybody against us today. There was even a cop on the sideline yelling at us and I said, 'Get out of our bench.' And he was like, 'Oh no, this is my area.'

"I couldn't believe the audacity some of the people had. Even their water boys didn't respect us."

Says guard Tom Thayer: "There is nothing worse than driving away from Green Bay after losing a game. Everybody is giving you the finger and you just have to accept that.

"And there is nothing more gratifying than pulling away from Green Bay after you've beaten the Packers, because the finger they give you just doesn't mean as much."

Favre Stopper

Maybe it was the thought of facing Brett Favre in another Bears-Packer game. "We're at a big disadvantage," said defensive coordinator Greg Blache. "They got Brett Favre and Ahman Green and we just got us and that's not a fair fight. We're a little bit out manned right here."

What would make it a fair fight, Greg?

"A restraining order."

Keep Your Head Down

There is no place in the world where the football experience is what it is at Green Bay's Lambeau Field. But keep your helmet on at all times and don't let your guard, or linebacker, down.

"I loved playing the Pack," says Mike Hartenstine. "That was my favorite field of all time. I loved coming out of the locker room, you'd be underneath the stands and they'd wheel those fences out to stop the people. They'd be throwing beer, pop, hot dogs, batteries on you, and you had to keep your helmet on and your head straight ahead. Then you got in the stadium and you felt like you were in the arena.

"It got real vicious when Forrest Gregg got up there because he and Ditka hated each other. You had to have your head on a swivel at all times because you knew people were coming. He coached it that way and probably more against the Bears."

Ditka-Gregg

Many believe that the Bears-Packers hatred was at its worst during the Mike Ditka-Forrest Gregg years. The two were fierce competitors and rivals from their days as players under Halas and Lombardi, but this went deeper and had none of the respect that usually comes between two individuals who were, as players, equals.

An incident in Gregg's first year as Packers coach, 1984, killed any chance of respect.

The Packers were leading 14-3 nearing halftime of the Aug. 11 exhibition between the two teams, which were at opposite ends of the NFL world. The Bears were on the brink of their epic run through the NFC Central and the Packers were down, which was why Gregg was hired—to restore the roar.

With 1:12 remaining, Gregg called a timeout, which was a violation of the "code" during preseason, but Gregg wanted to send a message to his own players that the Packers were now out to bury people. Normally coaches would let the time run out and get their players in the locker room healthy.

Ditka was outraged. He yelled at Gregg, who said his guys needed to work on their passing game. The rhetoric worsened and the two had to be restrained from going at each other. During the second half, Ditka's mood worsened and he had sideline shouting matches with defensive coordinator Buddy Ryan, too—all in a preseason game!

The Packers would win 17-10 and the era of bad feelings was in motion. The teams have never played each other in preseason since.

Shutout

Both the Bears and Packers had their times of dominating each other. "One year up in Green Bay, in 1949, against Tobin Rote, we didn't let them complete a pass," said Ed Sprinkle. "That was quite a feat to keep a team from completing one pass.

"The events surrounding the games were something. We played in the old City Stadium and the fans were right behind your bench, so I never took my helmet off. You might get a bottle.

"We stayed in the Northland Hotel downtown and then took a bus out to the stadium. They'd honk horns all night and try to keep you awake, but once I went to sleep, I was out."

The "Other" Bears-Packers Rivalry

George Halas and Curly Lambeau may have been among sports' greatest rivals—they faced each other in the first Bears-Packers game in 1920—but there was much, much more than a feud between them. There was also a special bond.

When a retired Lambeau came to Chicago without a ticket to the 1961 Bears-Packers game in Chicago, Halas told the *Chicago Tribune* that Lambeau was guaranteed a seat at that game, even if it had to be on the Bears' bench.

Halas served as an honorary pallbearer at Lambeau's funeral in 1965. Halas was among the strongest advocates behind the Packers getting a new stadium, urging Green Bay citizens in 1956 to build what would be named Lambeau Field. Lambeau had accepted Halas' IOU in 1932 when, at the peak of the Great Depression, the Bears couldn't cover the $2,500 guarantee to the visiting team for a game.

And it was Halas who helped push through the league's policy of sharing television revenue, without which small-market teams like the Packers might never have survived.

CHAPTER 13

AFTERTHOUGHTS

Once a Bear, Always a Bear

Even when members of the Bears family leave Chicago, they never really leave. "It was so much fun to come to work every day," says Dave McGinnis, who came in 1986 as the linebackers coach, left to become defensive coordinator and eventually head coach of the Arizona Cardinals and nearly returned as the Bears' coach.

"You had a talented group of players that had a mission and that had a huge amount of personality. And the city was embracing that whole team. It was electric every day.

"We had so many personalities in every corner you looked. On Saturdays the players would bring their kids and their dogs and whatever up to practice for the workout and they'd take the kids up and throw them in the dryer or the whirlpool and the kids having a great time. It was a great feeling around there, it really was."

* * * *

"I loved playing with those guys because everybody came to play," says Mike Hartenstine. "The first time I met Jauron and his coaching staff at the fan convention, I told them, you don't even have to win in Chicago for people to love and appreciate you. Just beat the shit out of people when you play them. They'll embrace you here. That's how it was. That's how it still is and probably always will be."

* * * *

"I had an opportunity to go play in the USFL with the Chicago Blitz and George Allen," says guard and Joliet native Tom Thayer. "The reason I signed with the USFL was to stay in Chicago, because you never know where you're going to go in the NFL. Then two days later they have the NFL draft and I find out I'm drafted by the Chicago Bears.

"It was a great experience playing for George Allen and with some of the teammates that I played with in the USFL played in the NFL. But there's nothing like playing for the Bears. Nothing like it."

* * * *

"I'll stay in Chicago," tackle James "Big Cat" Williams said after his release by the Bears. "This is where my wife is from, where my son was born, and where so many good things happened for me. This is home now."

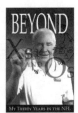